PRAISE FOR BEYOND EGO

"Thor thoughtfully unravels the significance of empowering leadership when we put our ego to the side, unlocking purpose and potential which cultivates the contributions of others."

IAN SMITH,
FORMER CEO OF BMW FINANCIAL SERVICES USA & THE AMERICAS

"If you are looking for an inspiration to grow as a person or to become a more conscious leader, this is the book for you. In *Beyond Ego*, Thor has combined insights from his spiritual and business experience and come up with a formula that can help leaders and others become a better version of themselves. I got to know the Inner Compass during a leadership training a few years ago, and it has truly helped me on my journey to look deeper within, become more conscious and lead with respect."

HELGA HALLDORSDOTTIR,
HEAD OF HR AT ARION BANK

"Thought-provoking and life-changing in many ways, *Beyond Ego* is a must-read for all aspiring leaders."

MARK SIVA,
SENIOR VICE PRESIDENT AT MIELE

"Trust is the foundation on which success is built. *Beyond Ego* explores unconscious behavior, bringing forward the basic principles we all instinctively know to be right but still have forgotten. It encourages you to reflect and draws on purpose-led leadership."

VAISHALI AHUJA,
HEAD OF HR, BMW JAPAN

"Changing the world begins by transforming our inner world. When we drop from our heads to our hearts and figure out what we really care about, we can craft our life compass. Thor provides you with effective guidance for that lifelong journey."

HALLA TOMASDOTTIR,
CEO OF THE B-TEAM

"In Chinese we say: we can conquer the world with only a few chapters of the book of Confucius. Likewise, I want to say: we can navigate the course of life with only a few chapters of the *Beyond Ego* book. Because, stuck inside our ego, we cannot find our inner compass, but if we can grow beyond our ego, we can find our inner compass."

GUO WEI,
LEADERSHIP COACH & TAI CHI TEACHER IN CHINA

"I loved *Beyond Ego*. It's refreshingly down-to-earth for the topics it covers and it's beautifully written. It's a book I'll certainly turn to again for its exercises, frameworks and stories."

SVEINN HRÓBJARTSSON,
CO-FOUNDER OF BREATHE

"If you want to take your leadership to the next level, then this is the book for you."

ASGEIR JONSSON,
CEO & OWNER OF LIFE WITHOUT LIMITATIONS

"This book is right on time for the shift in leadership towards purpose, people and planet. Thor has written an inspiring guide for finding and following one's own Inner Compass, leading us towards more human-centered and sustainable leadership."

DR. FRANK SCHLEIN,
CEO OF CRIF GMBH

"Sustainable development needs to become an integral part of business. It is the answer to the next generation's call for a green future. We have to find new ways of doing things as we head down those new paths. This book provides insights of how business leaders need to develop as persons and leaders to be successful in this better new world ahead of us."

HÖRÐUR ARNARSON,
CEO OF LANDSVIRKJUN (ICELANDIC POWER COMPANY)

"Thor introduced me to the journey to "my inner self" via "the Inner Compass" during a leadership program some 7 years ago. We continued to work together in coaching sessions, and it has been an extremely helpful and stimulating journey exploring values and purpose, both personally as well as in my leadership."

JOACHIM HERR,
CHIEF RISK OFFICER BMW BANK GMBH

"If you are looking to improve as a leader and at the same time become a better person, this is the book for you. Compassionately written, it shares convincing leadership theories supported by scientific evidence, inspiring stories and practical exercises. It brought tears to my eyes in its serenity ... and a smile to my face with its sincerity."

JONINA LARUSDOTTIR,
DIRECTOR AT EFTA SURVEILLANCE AUTHORITY

"Leadership has become one of the most mystified and crowded topics. *Beyond Ego* is the guide for every leader to go straight to the core of leadership, and to what matters most and can be most painful: you. Understanding who you are and how you connect this to the purpose of your business is key to being an authentic leader—today and every day."

MARC MAKOWSKI,
VP INNOVATION PORTFOLIO - ADIDAS

"In the current VUCA (volatility, uncertainty, complexity, and ambiguity) world leaders should help to identify values and purpose for their employees. Aligning to the organization's values and purpose will create a deeper sense of meaning, greater employee satisfaction, psychological safety and retention. *Beyond Ego* has captured insightful and practical ways to raise the awareness level of leaders. This must-read book gives you practical tools and practice exercises, which help to transform the self into a humble leader: one who leads beyond ego.

KRISHNA REDDY,
TECHNOLOGY LEADER, CUMMINS TURBO TECHNOLOGIES LIMITED

THE INNER COMPASS OF CONSCIOUS LEADERSHIP

BY THOR OLAFSSON
WITH SASHA ALLENBY

BEYOND EGO

THE INNER COMPASS OF CONSCIOUS LEADERSHIP

THOR OLAFSSON

WITH SASHA ALLENBY

New Leadership Press Publishing 2022

Visit www.beyondego.com for more details.

Front cover design by Kate Tuck

Thor Olafsson's Photo by Thomas Langer

Inner Compass Book Illustrations by Erla Maria Arnadottir

Edited by Lois Rose

Book design by Hossein Karimzadeh

ISBN

For the print book:	978-1-7397862-0-5
For the e-book:	978-1-7397862-1-2

THIS BOOK IS DEDICATED TO

MY WIFE SVAVA BJÖRK & OUR CHILDREN TÓMAS LOGI,
HINRIK ORRI, HILDIGUNNUR ÝR, GABRÍELA RÓS, BELINDA MIST
& ADAM BERG. WISHING FROM THE BOTTOM OF MY HEART
THAT THEY MAY FOLLOW THEIR OWN INNER COMPASS THROUGH LIFE

CONTENTS

PART THREE

PART FOUR

PART FIVE

PART SIX

FOREWORD

Thor and I met in early 2015 when Thor was running a specific year-long leadership development programme for the BMW Group and it was here that I was first introduced to the Inner Compass.

I remember quite vividly a question he asked me in these early stages, which was "Why would someone choose to follow you as a leader?" Never an easy question to answer, but in our work together I found valuable answers for myself. I have found that the Inner Compass has helped me to understand myself, understand what is important to me as an individual and ultimately how I lead the business and lead the team.

Moreover, in the years since then, the Inner Compass, coupled with

Thor's uniquely passionate and authentic delivery style, has helped me to continually reflect and challenge myself in a structured and constructive way. As a coach, Thor's style is one of alarming openness, creating a relationship of absolute trust and safety, to allow the coaching sessions to really go deep when necessary. Calm and reassuring, yet challenging and meaningful.

In open and honest discussions, over an extended period of time, we have tackled a variety of topics together, ranging from business leadership to career design and also private life. In that context, Thor has skillfully coached me through a series of change programmes over the years, helping me to develop my own purpose, not just as a leader, but also to gain clarity for myself as to who I am, and ultimately what is important to me and for me.

The result for me is that I feel more confident in the business and life decisions that I am taking on a daily basis, knowing that those decisions play into a bigger picture and towards a meaningful purpose and existence.

Being myself, being authentic, humble, and vulnerable—these all help to build relationships with the people around me, help us to connect and complement each other, so that we don't just deliver great results for the business, but we continue to grow as individuals and as a team.

I had made my own personal notes for future reference and use of the Inner Compass which I refer to regularly, and particularly when I find myself defaulting back to old habits and practices, which I now understand to be defined as my ego.

This book has captured and documented the workings and, importantly, the principles and rationale behind the Inner Compass, acting as a comprehensive reference point—not just for myself, but for future readers.

As they work with the Inner Compass, readers have the opportunity to steer themselves through an open and honest journey which will lead them towards their inner core. And in this book, just as in my coaching sessions, Thor has been thoughtful, candid and vulnerable in his guidance along that journey, sharing how personal experiences have shaped his approach to life and leadership.

Mike Dennett, BMW Group Financial Services UK

INTRODUCTION

There is a common, unconscious behavior in business leadership that needs to be carefully examined. It stems from a millennia of us—as human beings—constantly looking out for danger and developing strategies to ensure our survival. Our thousands of years of fighting for scarce resources and looking out for the safety of "me and mine" have resulted in subconscious behaviors that affect the way that we behave on countless different levels, and in particular, impact the way that we lead others. These survival-based behaviors have meant that we've developed an ego-based leadership strategy. It's a default mode that makes us feel separate from others, and a mindset that unknowingly guarantees that we keep fighting to develop a safe and successful environment with an accompanying and constantly present undercurrent of fear that there is something we need to protect.

One of the main outcomes of this unconscious, scarcity-driven mindset—and the ego—based leadership that accompanies it—is that it can create working cultures that are built upon fear. Usually without realizing the motivation behind our actions, we lead with a "carrot-and-stick" mentality, which can inadvertently trigger our employees into fear-based behaviors. We complain about the lack of communication and collaboration between business units, unaware that our own leadership approach is causing our employees to operate from fear, and that from these fear-based states, they are less able to connect with others and collaborate. Without realizing the impact of our actions, we create teams that perform to reach their silo-based goals, often motivated by the fear of the consequences of what will occur if they don't. Mostly, without realizing it, we create a culture that prioritizes business targets, divides people into silos and even pitches our employees against each other, teaching them that their value is based solely on the outcomes they achieve. In doing so, we commandeer the earth's natural resources, pushing for short term gains, rather than longer term wins. These strategies might, indeed, be effective in the short term, and on the surface, they may appear to create the outcomes that we seek, but in the longer term, pushing our employees into subtle, fear-based patterns is counterproductive to the outcomes we desire.

Although these well-established and commonplace approaches have been practiced universally for decades in companies around the globe, a new type of leadership is emerging. It turns the current business leadership paradigm of fear-based motivation on its head, creating a dynamic approach that is more purposeful, compassionate and humane. This more evolutionary approach creates an environment where individuals and teams can flourish and thrive, removing unnecessary stress and fear from the workplace and creating an environment where employees feel respected, and can work more harmoniously towards a common goal.

This human-centered approach to leadership is something that we intuitively know to be right, but because of how strongly ingrained the deficit mindset is, we keep unconsciously gravitating towards the old ways of forcing outcomes. Yet ironically, the impact of a more conscious approach means that, across the board, teams perform much more effectively than they did when they were managed under ego-based leadership strategies and pressured into performing.

A call for this more conscious approach to leadership is being heard around the globe. A growing sector of the business leadership community has been collectively seeking ways to challenge the old methods, and what is being uncovered turns our previous notions of business leadership upside down. It calls us to question our whole perception of how we have been approaching management, and it challenges the conventional notion of what an effective leader is, bringing forward a new leadership style that is different to the core. This evolutionary new approach is calling us inwards, asking us to listen to our wiser inner selves rather than relying on the fear-based ego patterns that have previously been our driving force.

A MORE CONSCIOUS APPROACH TO LEADERSHIP

This new, more conscious approach to leadership begins with us as leaders. In order to dismantle the old approaches, we need to be willing to carefully look within ourselves and question many of the values that our old approaches were built upon. This is essential because this new paradigm of business leadership brings concepts such as compassion, forgiveness and humility into the workplace. You may have noticed that these concepts are gaining traction in the business world under banners such as "psychological safety," "power of vulnerability" and "employee engagement" and have been pioneered by the likes of Amy Edmondson, Brené Brown and William A. Kahn. They are also found at the heart of organizations such as The B Team (co-founded by Richard Branson and Jochen Zeitz and led by CEO Halla Tómasdóttir), which is an association of business leaders who are convinced that a Plan B is needed for our world; a plan where a more humane and sustainable approach to business leadership is prioritized.

However, if we haven't looked within and brought concepts such as consciousness to life within ourselves, we will not be able to genuinely bring them to life in the workplace. If we try to impose them on the old ways of business management, they seem awkward or out of place. If we treat them as another thing we have to fit into our current structures, they become a performance, and our employees can see that. Instead, we have to profoundly transform the way we show up as leaders, so that we can lead our teams with authenticity, truthfulness and trust.

MY LEADERSHIP BACKGROUND

I came to this understanding of conscious leadership through my work as a global leadership coach and master trainer. I've been exploring this work in over 30 countries for the better part of more than two decades, and in that time, I founded several companies in four different countries, before deciding to concentrate all my efforts on my group of Strategic Leadership companies. We currently have a team of over 40 executive coaches and leadership trainers in countries around the globe. We specialize in coaching senior teams on becoming conscious strategic leaders, as well as working individually with top-level executives. We work with CEOs and MDs, as well as managers who are being fast-tracked towards a higher level of responsibility. Our clients include BMW, Bertelsmann, Continental, Roche and Miele, to name but a few. We are called in, not only to work with company leaders, but also to work with whole teams and company ecosystems.

The success of the Strategic Leadership companies is built upon one vital premise. *We don't just teach conscious leadership as a concept, we ourselves actively try to live it as fully as we can*. This approach is our passion, and it guides us from our core. The outcomes of our approach can be seen in the performance of companies that have embraced our methods over a longer period of time. We've been working with companies that have been deeply touched by our enthusiasm for our approach, and we've seen the changes that have occurred when leaders have wholeheartedly embraced our methods. The outcomes can also be seen in the growth of our own company, which nearly doubled in size during the COVID pandemic, again by endeavoring to live our own practices. But it's essential to understand that *our growth is a side effect of our approach, and not the main feature.* It is our willingness not to be governed by fear, but rather to operate with a more conscious leadership approach that brings these results, and this has only been made possible by our team's willingness to go deeply within and examine the way we show up as leaders ourselves, time and time again.

For me personally, the lessons that I learned in conscious leadership didn't come easily, and like many of the executives that I've coached, I've been near both burnout and bankruptcy, as well as having gone through a divorce. But in my lowest moments, I asked the big questions and did the deep work—both personally and professionally—and much of the body of work that I am about to share with you is based on how I've overcome the challenges that I've faced, and transformed the way I show up as a leader myself. Before I undertook this work, I was an insecure overachiever with arrogance as my main cover. Today I try to be a humble learner, driven by my sense of purpose, rather than the need for approval or recognition. So this work is something I try to profoundly live and learn from every day, and it informs both my personal life with my wife and six children (I have three from my first marriage, and my current wife has three of her own), and how I show up as a leader for my own team.

Of all the leadership development work that I have explored and designed through the last 20 plus years, the body of work that is resonating by far the strongest with my clients and my team is the work on the Inner Compass, which I will present to you in this book.

INTRODUCING THE INNER COMPASS

The main purpose of the Inner Compass training is to raise the awareness levels of leaders, so that they can take their awareness inwards and manage from that place. This work enables leaders to gain a more thorough understanding of who they are, and of their inner selves, so that they can see how the way they show up with their teams has an immediate impact on their working environment. This work is designed so that leaders who take it on board and do the inner work become more conscious in their leadership roles, and transform their teams in the process.

The Inner Compass represents a deeper and more meaningful path to leadership than the conventional one often offered. The leaders that we work with today don't want another soft skills training. They also don't want to spend the rest of their lives working long hours and meeting targets without really understanding the deeper aim of why they are there. They are hungry for something more than experiencing their job as a sprint that starts early in the morning and often spans the best part of twelve hours in a day. They want to recognize the meaningfulness in their own lives and bring it to the workplace, so that they can support their employees to do the same.

The Inner Compass is for leaders at all stages of their career. We see a younger generation of leaders who are already more aware, and are questioning the old ways and seeking out the new. But we also see an older generation of managers who have begun to ask if there is a different way. Both groups are waking up and yearning for a more humane, evolved and sustainable form of leadership. And this is who the Inner Compass speaks to—those who have started waking up, asking the big questions and yearning for something more.

BECOMING AN INNER COMPASS LEADER

So, the Inner Compass journey begins with you being prepared and willing to question many of the old techniques and approaches to management that have likely been familiar to you. We start with an in-depth look into why you went into management in the first place. When I ask this question—whether in small groups or at large events—surprisingly few managers have thought about why they are in charge. Most of them began as experts and after having been in the company for a while, management seemed like the next career step. Often their new role came with more status, more money and a new car. But very rarely have they invested any real time in asking, "Why am I doing this?" I mean the *big why*, outside of helping your team reach company targets. We ask the question "If they had a choice, why would anyone choose you to lead them? What's the added value they got when they landed with you?" Most of the managers I work with haven't considered these questions very much, and when we actively start to ask them, it opens up the way for a more thorough dive into their leadership purpose and the motivation behind their role.

When I carry out an in-person Inner Compass Retreat, I always start out by asking my participants to imagine a certain scenario, so I'm going to do the same with you here now. Imagine you have the kind of boss who shares a lot of truth with you and asks the same of you. At the same time, you have no doubt that she has motivations that are driven by a deeply informed purpose. Her ego is under control, and she is able to be vulnerable, while still being strong. She is passionate about looking within, and has made a commitment to be a more conscious leader. If you had this person as a boss, would you trust her more? Everyone I ask this question to answers that they would. So the same goes for you. Are you willing to make the commitment to be this kind of leader, for yourself and for your team? Do you dare to stand naked before yourself and who you are? When you fall flat on your face are you humble enough to get back up and give it another go? These are the hallmarks of an Inner Compass leader—one who is choosing consciousness, operating beyond ego and able to lead a team from this place. And this is the outcome that you can work towards if you sincerely commit to the Inner Compass work.

THE FOUR SEGMENTS OF THE COMPASS

As you work through this book, you will encounter the four segments of the Inner Compass. This book is designed so that you go through the four segments in the order that they appear, as each segment builds on the last, and the process I will take you through is similar to the one that has been tried and tested with leaders that we coach, as well as with those who attend our retreats.

1. SETTING THE COURSE IN YOUR LIFE

The first segment is about setting a course for your life, understanding what is meaningful to you, and giving it the place that it deserves. This is where you will be able to fully determine the purpose behind your leadership role and align it with your company's purpose. Getting clear on your purpose—why you are there and what fuels you—will inform all the other elements of the Inner Compass, and it is the groundwork for the rest of the work we will do together.

2. MEETING YOUR EGO

The second segment is where we move into looking at how your ego can derail your purpose-driven intention. For clarification, when we talk about ego, we aren't referring to it in the Freudian sense. We're talking about the layers of patterns that were built up through your life experiences, particularly those that have become coping strategies that—for most people—are no longer conscious and in many cases, no longer represent the best version of who we are. So you set your purpose in the first segment, but your ego will tell you, "You have bills to pay. Deadlines to meet. A super demanding boss. Let's forget about being intentional and focus on the important stuff." In this segment you will learn that *you can't meet ego with force*. You can't willpower it away. Instead you will practice meeting it with humility and learn new ways to stay humble.

3. LETTING GO

The third segment is about letting go. The lessons in this segment will enable you to let go of who you used to be and who you are telling yourself that you are. The stories of who you believe you are—as a manager and in your life in general—deserve thorough introspection. In this section you'll decide what you want to keep and what you want to let go of, and this will impact you personally and professionally.

4. EMBRACING YOUR INNER SELF

The fourth segment is where you take a conscious leap into being informed by some of the higher qualities of humanity. You learn to embrace the fact that the wisdom of these higher qualities is already there and they are a part of your inner self. One of those qualities is gratitude, and this segment will invite you to step into a state of heartfelt gratitude. When gratitude is a guiding force in your life, it impacts everything you do. It's not just the kind of gratitude you feel when you say thank you to a team member for performing a task. It's that lip-quivering, 'tear in the eye' gratitude that we often feel for loved ones. We discover how to live and lead from this place, and a whole new kind of energy comes with that feeling when we do. We're more forward moving. We're more open. And we inspire the same in our team.

This segment also inspires more self-compassion—and compassion for others too. From this place you can deeply connect with those you lead and understand them from a human perspective. Earlier, I shared that compassion is gaining more traction as a viable concept in business. The challenge is that few of us know how to get there. With the groundwork that you will have done through the Inner Compass, at this stage you will not only create an environment of compassion within yourself: you'll create a compassionate working environment too. You will also learn how to create psychological safety for your team members. Vulnerability, diversity and inclusion, and psychological safety are among the emerging topics in business management, and with the work that you do in this segment, you will enable your team to feel safe so that they can thrive.

We'll then look at some common business scenarios so that you can bring the Inner Compass to life in your most challenging moments, whether it's implementing new strategies that require a lot of change, creating an open and transparent feedback culture, delegating projects, or planning and budgeting for the next year. With each challenge we will use the Inner Compass as an experiential path so that you can uncover what is possible.

What's essential about this Inner Compass work is that you likely won't just go around the Compass once, and then be done. It's designed so that each journey around the Compass is informed and impacted by the last. So once you go around the second or the third time, you'll start to see an exponential increase in the qualities and markers of conscious leadership—this approach is a lifetime dedication to self-discovery through the leadership role, and not a one-time shot.

This reminds me of a famous fable in martial arts. A martial arts student approached his master and asked seriously, "I dedicate myself to learning your art. How long will it take for me to reach the master rank?"

The teacher replied, "Ten years."

The student answered impatiently, "But I want to get to the master's rank faster. I will work hard, train every day, ten or more hours every day, if I need to. How long will it take then?"

The teacher thought for a moment and replied, "Twenty years."

In short, mastery of the Inner Compass will not come through forcing outcomes or trying to push impatiently towards conscious concepts such as compassion and humility so that you can tick them off your list. It will, instead, be informed by our willingness—mine and yours—to continually look inwards and use this work as a roadmap to boldly and bravely question everything that we have been taught about leadership so far, and to reinvent what's possible with each journey round. By the end of this book you'll not only have a blueprint for conscious leadership, you'll have the tools and practices necessary to transform yourself into a humble leader: one that leads beyond ego and is deeply respected by your team.

CONSCIOUS LEADERSHIP
LEADING BEYOND EGO

PART 1

CHAPTER 1
LEADING FROM BEYOND EGO

Is it possible that a future exists where the topic of human consciousness is a normal part of our daily business conversation? A world where—as business leaders—we have honed a heightened sense of self-awareness, which we use to make more conscious decisions in our workplaces, our homes, and in the wider world around us? A reality where, as conscious leaders, we are motivated by a purpose-driven vision and guided by clear strategy, creating a more sustainable business world? A place where we create environments for employees where they can not only feel appreciated as individuals, but where they can also know their own purpose and simultaneously operate as a meaningful part of the whole?

Although this approach has not yet been widely embraced by the corporate world at large, a growing number of managers are coming to the realization that conscious leadership is our most effective way forward. This more awakened leadership path is characterized by managers who are strongly connected to their core, and are able to lead with that core visible to their employees. They are able to embrace their own vulnerability, and express it with their strength still intact. They allow their team members to be vulnerable, and in doing so they create a psychologically safe workplace where new ideas are welcomed and encouraged, and mistakes are treated as learning opportunities. They are direct in their communication, but in a way that supports their team to grow, rather than cutting them down with fear. And most importantly, these managers are *no longer led by the usual attributes of their ego patterns*, but are instead, humble learners who are open to constructive criticism, allowing their teams to share in their growth edges and learn from their shortcomings too.

Expanding our own consciousness as managers is ultimately the key to developing these more sustainable and human-centered working environments. When we commit to growing our own consciousness as leaders, we create cultures where individuals feel acknowledged, at ease in the workplace, more engaged in their work, and more creative in their ideas. And although many of us may have assumed that these kinds of environments will make employees less productive, the opposite appears to be true. When leaders are transparent and open, when people feel truly appreciated as they are, when there's support for their personal growth and their weaknesses are treated with dignity, and when the cohesion between team members is prioritized and worked upon, we create effective and powerful teams who are more productive in the long run, and work more efficiently and effectively towards the outcomes that we are striving for.

In this opening chapter, we're going to explore how this more conscious approach of leading beyond ego challenges the current business paradigm, because often without realizing it, the majority of us run our organizations in a semi-conscious state. And we are going to look closely at what happens to us as leaders, and the teams that we lead, when we commit to leading beyond our egos.

RESISTANCE TO CONSCIOUS LEADERSHIP

I want to acknowledge that historically, it's been challenging to bring the subject of consciousness to the table in the business arena at large. In truth, most of us have been unconsciously taught that the *content* of what we create as managers is far more valuable than the *context* from which we lead. Collectively we've been trained to focus more on our results, and less on the environments we create to achieve those results. Most of us have not received an effective blueprint for developing ourselves as conscious leaders and creating a human-centered environment from which we can consciously lead. As a result, many of us have often unconsciously fallen into ego-based leadership patterns because we haven't been modeled alternatives.

Although I've been approaching the conversation of consciousness in a business setting for a good decade now, in the early days, when I was beginning to bring this work forward in a leadership context, I struggled to bring the topic of human consciousness into our conversations about business, and my clients had difficulty discussing it too. It seemed that—particularly when we talked about business strategy—there was no natural bridge into the topic of how to be a conscious human being *and* a business leader at the same time. When we did get into the consciousness aspect of leadership, it was usually in private conversations behind closed doors about following our purpose and doing something meaningful with our lives. Very rarely did we manage to raise these topics in group conversations, or in discussions with our teams. The corporate world can often demonstrate high levels of conformity, where many people give up on swimming against the current and instead just go with the flow. In honesty, it took me a long time to build the courage to publicly swim against the current, and there were many times when I gave up and went with the flow, stifling the calling to create a more conscious working environment for my team and going back to focusing on achieving short-term goals.

Over time, however, I began to connect the dots. I realized that people are naturally conscious beings, who have sometimes lost the ability to openly and fearlessly connect with other human beings. Sometimes, some of those very same people find themselves in management positions where they are expected to lead others towards success. With their human connection weak, blocked or lost, the fast-paced and fear-based business world can turn them into cold and tough decision-makers who function more like profit-driven management machines than heart-centered humans. Although they often get results, the downsides include short-term thinking, misalignment of priorities, low engagement levels and a seeming disregard for long-term sustainable thinking.

The catch is that, as managers, most of us have not been trained in what being conscious means, much less spent time thinking about it. When I start working with them, many managers will admit, "I don't have a meaningful vision that I communicate to my team. I haven't sat down and asked whether I am on the same purposeful journey as my company. I haven't given these things much thought. I don't see the true potential of my team: I inherited them. Strategy isn't my job. I just achieve my targets." Generally, managers have to deal with three circles: (i) the decisions they can make on their own, (ii) their circle of influence; ones which they can still influence but are outside of their circle of decision, and (iii) their circles of concern, which are often outside of their influence. Too many managers are drawn to the circle of concern which wastes both time and energy, without realizing that there are ways to impact the two inner circles, which could significantly change the way their teams and organizations function on a fundamental level.

The accompanying dissatisfaction, divorce rates, burnout and depression that come with the more common approach to management often add up to enough motivation for some of the more thoughtful leaders I work with to genuinely ask, "Is this the only way?" Many

of the managers my team and I work with have been privately asking themselves that question long before they start working with us, or have had glimpses of something more.

LOOKING WITHIN AS CONSCIOUS LEADERS

If we want to be more conscious as leaders, it probably comes as no surprise that we need to look deeply within ourselves and examine the inherited patterns that have been causing us to lead from a semi-conscious state, and operate from ego-based patterns. We can begin by becoming aware of who we are, where we want to go and why this journey is so vital to us. These kinds of questions are not necessarily commonplace in a conventional leadership context or asked with a strong enough intention.

Yet the strongest leaders that I have met know who they are. They know their strengths and actively apply them. They know their own values and take a firm stand on them. *They also know their own ego patterns and take responsibility for them*. As a result, they are more balanced and grounded individuals who are comfortable in their own skin, and from there they can join forces with like-minded people and strategize on the best way forward. When they know who they are as a leader, and what their purpose is, this passes down to their teams. The teams that they lead become more efficient, and they learn to stay focused on what matters. But we can only create these outcomes with our teams if we are prepared to look deeply within ourselves. Otherwise conscious leadership becomes another priority on our to-do list, and nothing really changes at the core. Rather than seeing conscious leadership as something that we do once and then move on, through developing heightened awareness, we can take a deep dive into looking at our ego patterns, become a constant witness to the growth of our own consciousness and discover how this impacts our roles as managers.

A DEEPER DIVE INTO THE EGO

We have established that when we refer to ego, we are not talking about it in the Freudian sense. Instead we are defining ego as the part of us that has a role of keeping us safe. We can see conscious leadership as a kind of spectrum where, on one end, we are completely lost in our ego and our patterns, and ruling from a place of fear. And on the other end, we are ultimately free from ego, which translates into being conscious of our actions, humble and compassionate, and willing to learn from our mistakes so that we can grow.

In the chapter on truth, which follows this one, we will begin to explore how these ego patterns started developing in early childhood. All our negative experiences, traumas and rejections, each time we were scolded or belittled, every disappointment and every wound within: *It is around these that our ego forms.* We'll discover how our ego is not working against us, but rather is the way that we learned to deal with our experiences in life, the story we tell ourselves about who we are, and the coping strategies that we formed as a result. So in many ways it's the manifestation of the pain and hurt within us, and many of our reactions come from the tiny child inside us that has yet to heal.

There are many different ways of reacting to fear and danger, but each of us usually settle on one or two strategies, which embed in us to become a guiding force. Some children withdraw and hide in their room, then later in life when those same adults are faced with a challenge, you'll see them once again fleeing when something goes wrong. Others go into denial, and then when an issue arises in adulthood, they will refuse to take responsibility, and you'll see them projecting the blame onto someone else. Then there are those who learned to respond with aggression. We'll see them flare up in their adult life as though a switch has been flicked. We'll also see the perfectionist, keeping everything in the tightest of orders and trying to control their outer world so that they can feel safe within. And you'll see the people-pleasing diplomat, the one who does right by everyone at the expense of their own well-being because if they are the favorite, then there can't be any threat. You'll see the goth, the punk, the rebel, the one that won't follow anyone else's rules and then later in life, they will struggle to fit in. Then there's the researcher, the know-it-all who has all the answers, and fights to be right because that's how they managed to stay safe as a child. The facets of this survival mechanism are countless, but they all have one thing in common: they served the vital purpose of keeping us safe when we were young and we still unconsciously play by their rules when we sense danger in the present day.

WHY WE HANG ON TO EGO PATTERNS

In a way—and this is the challenging piece for all of us—*if we are good at operating from a particular ego pattern, it doesn't necessarily feel like a defensive strategy. In fact, it feels more like a winning formula.* We've likely been using it to get by for a long time, and it has produced many payoffs in our lifetime. "It's been my success strategy and I hang on to it because it got me to where I am" is a common response I hear when I challenge managers on their ego strategies in my coaching sessions with them. This is why we feel so reluctant to let go of them. But if we look closely, *the strategies that we thought were our winning formulas are getting us only so far in life.* And if we are willing to examine them, then we open up ourselves—and our teams—to so much more.

HOW OPERATING FROM EGO AFFECTS OUR TEAMS

If we gather people in one place such as an organization, and we examine how the individual ego strategies are working together, we start to see how ego can be counterproductive to a conscious working environment.

Imagine everyone in one workplace who is fixed in their ego strategies. Let's just say the CEO is highly demanding, results-driven, aggressive, and super smart, and she starts to put performance pressure on the organization. Everyone's defense mechanism is activated because they don't want to be the ones to fail her, and each team member starts to act from their own definition of fear. What manifestations do we see in this scenario? We see one team member hesitating to make bold decisions, because what if it goes wrong? We see another being reluctant in terms of volunteering for something new and risky. We see different ego manifestations clashing in meetings. The one who is the perfectionist clashes with the one who needs to be the winner. The one who hides suddenly disappears, and we can't resolve issues because they are not there. We see infighting and disagreements. Because there is no environment of psychological safety, nobody operates from their highest levels of creativity or insight: when individuals are so stuck in their identification of ego patterns, they often can't see that there's another way.

HOW PSYCHOLOGICAL SAFETY IMPACTS TEAMWORK

In contrast, if we create psychological safety in the workplace, and build teams without ego as the guiding force, we see that individuals within those teams start to act in extraordinary ways. There is an element to our human nature that, when fostered and nurtured, can mean that we operate from our greatest potential. This element was explored extensively in Google's 5-year study, which they codenamed "Project Aristotle." The study was based on the famous Aristotle quote which states, "The whole is greater than the sum of its parts."

The study followed 180 teams with the aim of asking what makes a team efficient and effective. In an article on Google's re:Work site, they defined the difference between a work group and a team:

- **Work groups** are characterized by the least amount of interdependence. They are based on organizational or managerial hierarchy. Work groups may meet periodically to hear and share information.
- **Teams** are highly interdependent—they plan work, solve problems, make decisions, and review progress in service of a specific project. Team members need one another to get work done.[1]

The study measured effectiveness based on four parameters, which included (i) executive assessment of the team, (ii) how the leaders evaluated the team, (iii) how the actual team members evaluated the team they were in, and (iv) the sales performance of the team. It also measured the dynamics of effective teams, and it highlighted the five areas where effective teams flourished. These included:

1. Psychological **safety - particularly** an individual's sense of the consequences of taking risks and speaking up.
2. **Dependability - those** teams who could be relied on to complete work in a timely manner.
3. Structure and **clarity - the** understanding of expectations and the creation of clearly set goals that could be followed.
4. **Meaning - a** sense of purpose in the work.

5. **Impact - the** sense that their work is making a difference.[2]

Psychological safety came out as number one in this study. The term was championed by Harvard Professor of Leadership and Management Amy Edmondson, whose TedXHGSE talk on "Building a Psychologically Safe Workplace" summarizes how to build it with three core components. Firstly, "Frame the work as a learning problem, not an execution problem." This approach "Creates the rationale for speaking up." Secondly, "Acknowledge your own infallibility" (as a leader). Say simple things like 'I may miss something that I need to learn from you.' Thirdly, "Model curiosity. . . Ask a lot of questions," which "creates a necessity for hearing voice."[3]

If we think about psychological safety: it means I can speak my mind on the team without any fear of being judged. I don't need to play political games or be cautious about showing my hand, because I know my opinion is valued and respected, even if not everyone agrees with it. And if we think back to all the ego strategies that a conventional business scenario can trigger in us, we see that this kind of approach disables the ego mechanism in everyone on the team, because they are no longer operating from uncertainty. Being the best, being the strongest, being the people-pleaser: these are all games that no longer need to be played here. Instead, "We appreciate who you are; we acknowledge your perfectness as well as your imperfections. You are a good team member. You are enough; you are right for us." And then the ego starts to see that the game it is playing is pointless, because its strategies aren't needed in an environment of this nature.

We also add another element here, which is vulnerability. This goes hand-in-hand with psychological safety. In Brené Brown's extensive body of research on this matter, in her viral 2010 TedX talk, and also in her book *Dare to Lead*, she questions the self-interested and self-protecting behaviors of conventional workplaces, and instead, champions the power of vulnerability in a leadership context.

In terms of leading a team, if you want everyone to be the best version of themselves, you need to lead them beyond ego to a place where vulnerability and psychological safety are the norm in the workplace. Which means you have a responsibility, as a leader, to be the one who finds ways to put people at ease. You can do that by being truthful, sharing your higher purpose, operating intentionally, being humble, and developing compassion, all of which we will be exploring throughout this book.

We see further evidence of the impact of this approach on teams in the aforementioned article on re:Work that summarizes Google's Aristotle study. We learn that a team of superstars did no better than a team of average people. In the team of average people, because their egos weren't in the way, they could be vulnerable and progress. The *New York Times* also published an article on the study entitled "What Google Learned From Its Quest to Build the Perfect Team." While the article on re:Work showed the statistics behind the study, the *New York Times* article showed the human elements of what happens to a team when we approach working with it in this way.

In his book *The Five Dysfunctions of a Team: A Leadership Fable*, Patrick Lencioni shares a story which highlights why even the best teams struggle. He shares a leadership model with action steps that overcome these hurdles, pointing out that vulnerability-based trust is absent in dysfunctional teams. He comes to the same conclusion as the aforementioned studies—that psychological safety is key to the effectiveness of teams.

INTRODUCING THE INNER COMPASS AS A PATH THAT LEADS BEYOND EGO

Now that we've established that it's more effective to lead our teams from beyond ego, for the rest of this book I'm going to present a path—the Inner Compass—that can guide you towards being the most efficient and effective version of yourself, both at home and in the workplace. It's an approach that, when consistently and sincerely applied, could ignite the most potent qualities of leadership, and support you to become a world class leader. It's a system that enables you to show up in even the most challenging business scenarios with complete presence, and solve problems from a place of consciousness and awareness.

The Inner Compass that I present to you is the "how" behind developing your leadership model, and you prioritize your leadership development so that you lead beyond ego. It's an experiential path towards self-discovery and enhanced connection with your inner self.

But the challenge is that you cannot just think your way through it. You have to experience it.

This path is one of individual growth and reflection. We're going to challenge your self-perception and the stories that you are telling yourself so that we can get to the truth of who you are. We're going to support you to set a meaningful purpose and operate intentionally. We're going to look at where your ego trips you up and derails your intentionality. We're going to develop your humility, while supporting you to let go of any ego patterns or past regrets that are keeping you from showing up fully present as a leader. And we're going to move into the higher qualities of leadership such as compassion and gratitude, so that the very tenets of your management path will significantly change. You'll move into being a more conscious leader who is guided as much by intuition as you are by logical thinking. You'll develop yourself as a fully conscious human being who is operating in the context of leadership.

JOURNEYING AROUND THE COMPASS

Below is a visual of what the Inner Compass looks like, and all the elements that we are going to be developing.

Starting with truth, we are going to explore all these eight elements; but we won't be dealing with them in isolation, because they are all interrelated, and each element impacts the other. We start by going clockwise from truth to purpose, then to intention, humility and trust.

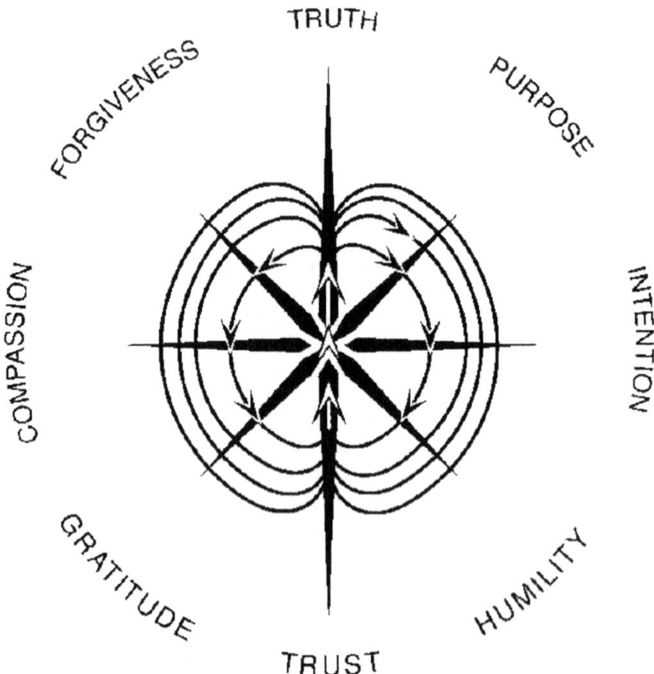

Once we get to trust though, we shoot back up the vertical axis to truth, and work our way counterclockwise through forgiveness, compassion and gratitude. So our journey around the Compass forms an infinity sign which looks more like this:

The Compass can be seen as an infinity symbol (like the figure 8 on its side), and it is not one where we go around once and then we are done. We go around it over and over again, and each time we do, we grow more. You make a small 8 the first time. But with the second, third and fourth cycles, the 8 has grown, and you start to feel the effect of shedding the layers, and each time you get closer to your core—the real you that exists beyond all the patterns and layers that have built up over time. And when you lead from this place, you become both present to all that exists in each moment—free from past mistakes and injustices—and fearless of what is to come.

Now that we've touched upon the benefits of conscious leadership, and the need to lead from beyond our egos, we're going to move into the first segment of the Inner Compass, which is truth and purpose, where we'll set a course for your life. This includes discovering the truth about who you really are and setting a course for your life based on that truth.

FIRST SEGMENT
SETTING THE COURSE IN YOUR LIFE

PART 2

CHAPTER 2 TRUTH

The biggest dirty little secret in business is the lack of candor. **Jack Welsh**

I Many of us would like to believe that we are guided by truth, and that we are truthful to our inner core. But in a conventional business scenario, truth is not necessarily a guiding value. When we peel back the layers—particularly in corporate settings—we start to see the many different ways that the truth is manipulated and distorted.

For the Inner Compass, truth is the starting point. We begin with truth because it's the foundation for all of the other elements of the Compass. When I did my first big speech on the Compass, one audience member told me, "Interesting concept, but you only need truth and trust." A religious guy that I presented this material to also shared, "In the middle of the Compass you should have faith; it's the combination of truth and trust." So you can call these elements the heartbeat of the Compass. It's the core that sits at the center of everything that you do.

When we look at truth from an Inner Compass perspective, we are really looking at three elements. These are: truth for your corporation, truth for your team, and truth for yourself. It probably won't surprise you to learn that truth for yourself is the starting point for the work we are going to do, because once you get aligned with your own truth, the way you interact with the truth for your team and the corporation that you operate within will radically transform.

In this chapter , therefore, we'll look at truth as your starting point for the work that we are going to do together. We'll examine why corporations and teams aren't always truthful, and how this lack of truth impacts the whole workplace. Then we'll turn to you and begin to uncover your own truth. Once you have become sincerely truthful with yourself—and uncovered the parts of yourself that have been unknowingly hiding from the truth—you will show up differently for your team and your organization, and it will sincerely impact the way that you operate as a leader from here on in.

THE DIFFERENT WAYS THAT ORGANIZATIONS AREN'T TRUTHFUL

Most organizations would like to think that they have a core value of truth. This value goes hand-in-hand with trust, particularly the trust that each team member is given within their organization. In most conventional setups, the senior management teams would likely argue that trust is widely given to the majority of individual team members within the organization. But when we look closely, we can see that this is not usually the case. Trust is not as commonly given as managers would like to think. This intrinsic lack of trust creates a distortion of truth, which becomes an insidious and unspoken barrier to honest communication.

One well-known example is Volkswagen's emission scandal where they knew their cars were emitting more pollutants than were officially communicated, and intentionally covered it up.

In another example, Enron hid billions in dollars of debt in order to indicate favorable performance and boosted their share price by knowingly using misleading accounting and overly optimistic revenue projections.

These examples show how corporations sometimes develop their own identity or personality that may be based on a lack of—or distortion of—truth. As they ruthlessly drive for financial performance, their employees' ego patterns are activated, causing them to have a short-term focus on "my survival and my success." This temporarily clouds the judgment of people who may seem to lack ethics on the surface or seem to be only financially motivated. But often when you dig deep into these individuals you will find someone who essentially (when they stop and think about it) wants the best for the planet and everyone living on it. In other words, their survival behaviors distort their truth.

Then there are all the "smaller" incidents within a corporation where truth is withheld in order to better control a situation. These are also fear-based, and include not revealing profit margins to employees, not telling employees about the actual purpose of a change project when it is really about cost cutting, and hiding gender-based salary inequalities.

There is a German saying: "Trust is good but control is better." This puts the value of controlling employees over the value of living in truth. It creates an "us that know," and a "them that don't know," and unconsciously, by operating in this way, we create division in our companies. The "us that know" are obviously the owners of information that others do not have access to. This gives them power, which also gives them the illusory feeling of safety. This is a key example of ego-based behavior governed by a deficit-oriented mindset. I believe that these kinds of behaviors are among the reasons that Jack Welsh called the lack of candor "the biggest dirty little secret in business," and this lack of candor is the big elephant in the room.

THE DIFFERENT WAYS THAT TEAMS AREN'T TRUTHFUL

When organizations aren't truthful, it creates a similar situation within the teams themselves where, for example, nobody dares to disagree with their manager or gives them feedback about it. In too many business scenarios, managers are the first to speak up, and when they do so, they influence everyone with their ideas. Usually all the team members play along, and nobody dares to be truthful enough to point this out. So we have managers influencing team members, sometimes stifling their creativity because nobody is speaking their truth. In short, everybody ends up playing a role. They get in line. They play their part. And while they do, the truth gets stifled and distorted even further.

An example of this can be seen in a CEO I once coached. He would bypass management layers to get information from the shop floor, undermining the authority of the managers in between and causing confusion amongst employees. He didn't realize how much damage this was doing, because it took a year for anyone on his team to dare to give him feedback on this matter. A behavior that might have been justifiable in a crisis had become commonplace, and this in turn caused untold damage to the integrity of his team. Nobody spoke their truth for a year, because they were afraid of the consequences if they did. Eventually he took the feedback from his team (which had to be repeated several times over a few months before it was integrated) and he significantly reduced "hunting for data" in this manner. He was not able to completely stop (nor was that entirely necessary), but he significantly improved, to the point where his managers felt trusted again.

Beyond not feeding back to managers, when it comes to teams, we can see a multitude of different behaviors where the truth is covered up. Some examples are:

- Moving cost and/or revenues between business years to boost bonuses.
- Knowing about a problem and not flagging it, so as not to jeopardize status and/or a bonus.
- Not disclosing all information to other teams in order to look better than them in comparison.

Unfortunately, these kinds of scenarios are too common in corporations, and they do untold damage. The outcome is that if someone on a team is not happy with the way things are working, it's unlikely that they are going to speak up. What's even worse is that, instead, they may gossip with someone in the cafeteria and express their shock and dismay about their manager, but there is often a block so they cannot be directly truthful to their manager. The end result is that this lack of candor leads to dysfunctionality. It creates communication barriers which naturally arise if we can't be truthful, because we're worried about someone's reaction.

Many of these challenges are based on how we were raised. If our mom put the Sunday meal on the table, we likely felt we had to say that it was good, no matter what we really thought. And sometimes we were trained to lie directly. If someone called our home and our parents didn't want to speak to them, we were told to pretend that they were not home! So most of us were not raised to be candid. Yet both senior managers and their team need to be truthful, in order for their organization to develop.

Much of the problem also lies in what was highlighted earlier: that organizations in general are governed by carrot-and-stick methods which reward us if we are doing well, and punish us if we are not. The concept of psychological safety isn't present when we rule in this way, and because we haven't yet discovered how to create a psychologically safe environment for those we lead, it's not very common for employees to tell their CEO that they are micromanaging, or that everyone is following them like lemmings. The pattern, instead, is for individuals to wait for the CEO to speak up and then follow what they say, while quietly pressing their own ideas down. Conversely, the CEO typically gets annoyed because of a lack of creativity and ideas in their team, and so it becomes a vicious cycle.

THE WAYS THAT WE AREN'T TRUTHFUL WITH OURSELVES

So far we've acknowledged that in many ways organizations and teams aren't truthful, but we need to take a closer look at our own relationship with truth too. This is a sensitive topic, and one that we need to take care to unpack with the respect that it deserves. Most of us want to believe that truth is a core quality, and any suggestion that it isn't can create a defensive reaction. Yet if we understand and are prepared to acknowledge that the majority of us are fundamentally truthful, but that we also learned some common strategies and coping mechanisms which weren't necessarily guided with truth at the core, we can begin to have a completely different relationship with our own truth. Even those that I have coached who have been initially defensive or skeptical about getting closer to their own truth, have welcomed the relief that it brings when we really get to the core of this issue.

Let's say we acknowledge that we may have been managing in a way that means our team members can't be candid with us. If we are then able to look closer at this as a possibility, we can start to ask, "What does that say about my relationship with myself? Am I really being truthful with myself to my core?" This is where it gets both fascinating and tricky, and we start to begin our real journey with the truth. We may feel we are being truthful to ourselves. But in reality, do you really know who you are, or—like most people—*are you telling yourself a story about who you are?* What have you inherited because of the way you were brought up? Is it possible that there is more below the surface than the story of who you believe that you are? These are challenging questions for all of us, and ones we will work with as we progress through this chapter.

WHY WE AREN'T ALWAYS TRUTHFUL WITH OURSELVES

It probably won't surprise you to learn that much of our inability to be truthful with ourselves and others is a pattern that we learned early on. Most of us had situations in childhood—particularly ones that caused us emotional pain—which led us to create coping strategies. When a child is faced with a situation that they don't have the emotional capacity to deal with, and the adults around them don't have the emotional intelligence to guide that child to process what happened, that child is going to need to form coping mechanisms of their own. But given the limited knowledge and resources available to that child, those strategies aren't likely to be the most conscious or effective forms of processing either. In one way or another, we all had to adapt our behavior to deal with our surroundings. However, if any of these strategies are even the slightest bit effective, that child is going to grow into an adult that reverts back to those strategies time and time again. Before we know it, our brain and our nervous system have wired to create a way of being in the world that is familiar and natural to us. And even though we may have optimized and evolved other aspects of our life, these strategies that we learned when we were under stressful situations while younger will keep repeating in our adult life. If you have any kind of awareness of behaviors that seem outdated but that you keep repeating—either professionally or personally—then you will know what I am referring to here.

I'm thinking about one of my former clients, Johnny, as I write this now. He was the middle child of five brothers in a working-class family, and there was not much money to go around. Early on, Johnny began to be guided by fear. He had the fear of not being important. He was also afraid of being bullied by the two older brothers. He was especially fearful of the bullying of his oldest brother, and learned strategies of humor to deal with the second oldest one. The one below him in age, he bullied himself. The youngest brother, he both bullied and protected. The bottom line of his behavior was that the strategy he used in his approach to people was based on whether he felt safe or afraid. In addition, he adopted his parents' scarcity mentality that there was never enough to go around. Without knowing it, he took these character traits from childhood with himself into adulthood. Even though he was a successful manager in a corporation, he had a subtle, underlying feeling that he wasn't important enough. He also brought some of his scarcity mentality to the workplace, with a constant feeling that there weren't enough financial resources, even when the company was thriving. The challenge for Johnny—like all of us—is that these patterns were not overtly recognizable. They sat beneath the surface as a subtle feeling that governed everything he said and did.

Another example can be seen in a CEO that I worked with who had a very strong character, and was perhaps even one of the smartest people I have ever met. He had an unparalleled understanding of the economy and could apply this understanding very effectively in his role as CEO. However, he did have one shortcoming which was highly destructive: a short fuse that caused him to shoot back too quickly, and this had an extremely negative impact on his team. The challenge is, when a powerful CEO is very good at fighting, it creates a lot of friction in the team. Some of his team fought back and he either respected them or threw them out of the team. But a lot of his team became subservient, and as they were operating from a place of fear, he wasn't able to get the best from them. They avoided all unnecessary risk, hid uncomfortable topics from him and shifted responsibility to others so that they wouldn't have to take the fall. When we dug deeper, there was a personal reason behind this CEO's behavior. As a child he was massively bullied when he went to school. He was a very hardworking, intelligent, straight A student, and he was ostracized by his peers for his singular intelligence. And whenever he got bullied, he always fought back. When I coached him he was 50, and looking at a long, prosperous career, but he still had that short fuse. Inside him there was still a trace of that 10-year-old who very quickly fought back. And that was still his strategy. Whenever he was challenged on the job, he perceived it as a personal attack and the old pattern was triggered. Part of his truth about who he was included facing that little child who lived inside of him. Until he dealt with that trauma, he would continue to repeat the same patterns. So the truth about us is—and this has been said many times because it rings true for us at our core—we are like onions. We have all these layers, and we create a persona that is acceptable to the world, while underneath we have a multitude of strategies that aren't necessarily serving us. If these inner layers are still hurting, even if only subconsciously, they can be influencing the outer layers more than we would care to admit. We have to face the fact that these programs are running the show, and when we do, we can peel away the layers that are still hurting, and begin to reprogram the automated responses that are no longer serving us.

UNPICKING OUR PATTERNS SO WE CAN GET TO THE TRUTH

I once worked with Arthur, the head of quality for a number of plants. At that time, one of his tasks was to go to all the different plants in his company and show them a new way of increasing the quality levels.

But every time he met a new plant manager, he found himself hitting a wall.

One of the things that I often do when I work with individuals is take them through a personality test from the Gallup Organization. On this test, strengths such as analytical, command, intellectual, self-assurance and achiever came up as key elements of his personality. Although these are obviously strengths, we took some time to look at the shadow sides of these traits. "What did that look like when you were a kid?" I asked him. He shared that as a kid, his grades were outstanding, and the other kids called him "the wise guy," but it was used in a derogatory sense. I asked, "Is it possible that 'the wise guy' is accompanying you into these meetings today?" He agreed that it was. We called this software that was no longer serving him "the wise guy," and acknowledged how much that program was getting in his way. He started to remind himself of how that software was running the show, and he did so many times a day, each time gently asking his subconscious to work on a new piece of software that would respond better (without consciously entering into a logical problem-solving type of thinking on the topic). Then one evening, a friend of his asked him to go to a lecture. He went, but once there, he wasn't really listening: he'd already decided that the lecture wasn't for him. Then in the middle of it all, the lecturer said "I'm OK, you're OK," and he snapped to attention. It felt like the lecturer was speaking directly to him. When he shared this with me, he also told me, "That's the name of the new software." When I asked him to elaborate he said, "It's really simple: everyone is educated and competent and

I am too. That means I am OK and they're OK. I can just speak to them on their level. I do my little mantra now and the meetings are very different."

What Arthur discovered is that there are little switches in us that mean that we can let our younger selves—who have often been running the show—understand that we don't need their tactics anymore. If we are willing to put in the work and uncover these patterns, it completely changes the way that we show up professionally and personally. *But we have to get to the truth of them first.*

The challenge comes when we discover the truth, but don't want to let go of the persona that we have created. On some subconscious level—especially when we've benefited from it—we can find ourselves holding on to that persona we've created. I've had managers tell me, "Why should I make excuses for who I am?" and subsequently turn the arguments to fit the story they are telling about themselves.

I have also had clients say, "If I let go of all these things, who am I?" But if we can get beyond the fear, it's actually quite exciting to discover who we are without any of these layers. Many of us have bought into the belief that life isn't easy, especially if we've been faced with certain challenges. These challenges can be as simple as turning into a teenager and not feeling smart or sexy enough. When we feel like we aren't enough, it brings scarcity thinking, which in turn, brings fear that triggers us into survival. We are born as innocent souls and then we enter into the world and get hurt and experience fear and lack, and from that experience, scarcity thinking is born. This especially occurs when there isn't enough kindness, love and care. We form beliefs and make conclusions from these experiences. We believe, because we perceive ourselves not to be tall, pretty, strong or powerful enough, that we are going to have less and that we have to fight for what we have. The more we believe this, the more layers of protection we put over the purity that we started out with. So the ultimate journey is to go from being born innocent, to losing sight of that being, to finding it again.

A STRATEGY FOR UNPICKING YOUR PATTERNS

In order to face and transform the truth about how we are showing up, we need to get to the stage where we say, "I can see the pattern. I can see how I developed certain behaviors. Do I want to keep them? Are they helpful today?" When we get to this place, we can start to work with some tools that enable us to reprogram the way we show up in the world, both in our leadership roles and in our everyday life.

There's a popular coaching method that can help you reprogram your reactionary behavior. Say, for example, you find yourself like our CEO in the story earlier, with a pattern of snapping back. You already know this is a powerful button and a lot of the time you are not quick enough to catch yourself, so you end up regretting it after the fact. (You can use this method for any of your reactionary patterns, but I'm going to focus on snapping back as I share this example here.) Think of a specific moment when this reactionary pattern happened, and bring that moment to mind. Let's assume that your mind recorded everything that happened. Now imagine a strip of film at 32 frames per second. Find the frame a fraction of a second before you said what you later regretted. Then ask yourself: "What was going through my mind at that moment or how did I feel just before I snapped?" Write down the thought and/or feeling. Now ask yourself, "Is this a recurring pattern or theme?" Most of the time when I ask someone this question, they say yes. So what we have established is that there is a certain behavior triggered by a thought or feeling. At some point in your life this was a helpful reaction, and that's how it got anchored into you. Think back to your childhood or teenage years. Where or when was this helpful? This software has served its purpose for all these years protecting you in some ways.

If you think back to when it was helpful, you were maybe 12 or 13 when this software was written and put in place, and you kept growing and getting into more challenging situations. And that old program, because it had some use, stayed there. You may need to rewrite the old piece of software, particularly if it has outcomes that you no longer desire. If there was a name for that old piece and what it does, what would that name be? Most of the time when I ask this question the name has a negative association, and it's usually something you want to get rid of or at least alter significantly. This program was written in the subconscious. So it needs to be remade there and reworked there so that you can move past it. The next step is to trigger your subconscious into working for you to come up with a new software piece. It's like you are developing an advertising campaign. And to start with, you are going to see the name of the old software program that you want to get rid of many times a day. You might put it on post-it notes, set a reminder on your phone or place it on the dashboard of your car, for example, so that you really bring the awareness of that program to your conscious mind.

Whenever you see your reminder, the thought or feeling should come up, and you ask your subconscious, "Please come up with a name for the new program, along with a sense of what the new piece does for me." And then you drop the idea. You can't do this consciously, but if you do it week after week, the subconscious gets that message that this is something to work on. Usually when you are not thinking about anything in particular, it pops up and you just know this is it: the new word. And then you anchor the new word so that it becomes part of who you are.

There are different ways to anchor the new word, and what works varies for each individual. A few tried and tested methods include:

- Tell a trusted colleague about the new anchor and ask them to look out for any signs that the new software program is running, and give you feedback.
- Set a reminder on your phone so that the word pops up as often as is feasible per day, and you can ask yourself how you are doing.

- Frame the new software name and hang it on your office wall, explaining to everyone interested what it means to you and what you are trying to accomplish (this one came from one of the senior managers I coached and the interaction with others around the anchor was a very effective method of instilling it for him).
- Do a short daily meditation on the new software and what it means to you. This one is my personal favorite, and it works by sitting with eyes closed and breathing in the new software name, while feeling it in your body. For this one to be effective, it helps to avoid conscious thinking and instead feel how the new software is impacting your life.

One method is likely to be more effective than another for you, and of course, you might find your own method of instilling it in your life.

LEADING FROM A PLACE OF TRUTH

Ultimately, the outcome of doing this work around truth will be that you get to a place—once these patterns are no longer running the show—where you start to experience a greater truth of who you are.

I want to take a moment to distinguish between this kind of truth, which is at our core when we remove the patterns and programs, versus the more current trend for "speaking our truth." Often the latter is used as a justification for the patterns that are already there. The work that we are doing, however, is to get beyond those patterns and lead with truth at our core.

Some people ask, "Will you ever really know what's true?" And perhaps we will never really know. Perhaps there are simply too many layers to be uncovered in one lifetime. But on the other hand, once you have been there, and really experienced more of your own truth, you definitely know. So even though truth is a challenging topic to handle—particularly for those of us who have been ruled by our patterns for, say, half a century or more—if we are brave enough to look within and face our truth, it provides us with the foundation to move forward in a new way: a direction that is unfamiliar to who we have been before.

And this reminds me of an encounter I had over 10 years ago with a spiritual teacher when this work was coming to me. I went to Abu Dhabi where I worked with Gita Bellin (who is widely acknowledged as a pioneer of the transformation revolution in human behavior). There was a moment when I was meditating with Gita when the truth section of the Inner Compass came to me. I also spoke with her about the Inner Compass at that time and I remember her telling me that it would take 10 years for it to truly come into fruition. I also recall my reaction at that time, "I will only have to wait 10 years!" To me, that was a short period of time in the grand scheme of things. Another thing that she said really struck me: "Just remember that those who speak don't know. Those who know, don't speak." The bigger the insight, the less need there is to speak it. The truth already is. So the truth of the Inner Compass is that it has never been rushed. For me it has been something that is grounded in truth, and that has expanded from that place.

As part of the exploration of our behavior patterns, we start to assess our lives, and the search for meaning begins. As we explore the truth about how our behavior patterns came about—and whether we want to keep them—we find ourselves going deep, and visiting places within ourselves that may be unfamiliar to us. Once we are in this place, we naturally begin to ask the bigger questions. Questions about the meaning of life, and what is meaningful to us. This focus becomes an alternative foundation to fear, upon which we can build new behavior patterns. We start to ask ourselves what our true purpose is, and our life takes on new substance and meaning.

CHAPTER 3
PURPOSE

Passion and purpose scale—always have, always will. Every movement, every revolution, is proof of this fact. **Elon Musk**

Purpose is the raw fuel for the Inner Compass. It's the passion and the fire behind *everything* you do. As a leader, it radiates through your every action and punctuates your every word. When you find a meaningful purpose—and it's something that inspires and engages you—people will sense that in you: you know where you are headed and why you are headed there, and this steadfastness and definiteness will emanate from you. It becomes a source of strength and energy for you, and a source of inspiration for all those who encounter you. When you are aligned with your purpose and operate with it as a guiding foundation, you have a completely different resonance in the world.

And as a leader, it's a significant part of what makes others want to follow you.

Throughout history, we've seen iconic leaders accomplish almost impossible feats, and when we see what those leaders have in common, it is always that they were highly aligned with a single, guiding purpose. Gandhi didn't have much more than a clear purpose built on fairness, respect and the desire for India to be an independent nation. His purpose was so strong he conquered an empire. Emmeline Pankhurst founded the Women's Social and Political Union in the early 1900s with the sole focus of ensuring that women had the right to vote. When Mandela was released from prison, his purpose of showing that all individuals are born free and equal in dignity and rights united a nation and ended apartheid. Rosa Parks catalyzed a racial revolution in 1950s Alabama by famously refusing to give up her seat to a white male on a bus. Churchill galvanized the British people with the purpose of defending his island to the last man standing in the Second World War. All of these leaders demonstrated how much can be achieved with a purpose-driven agenda.

Although all the above individuals were leading movements rather than companies and organizations, you can also discover a similar fire behind your purpose in the work that you do. As an Inner Compass leader, you work to become the best possible version of yourself and fearlessly stay true to that version under pressure. And part of that truth is committing to a purpose that is worthy to you, and ensuring that it guides you in everything you do. When people are led by a conscious leader, motivated by a purpose-driven vision, and guided by an intelligent strategy, we have a recipe for a more sustainable and successful world.

We can summarize this power of purpose in our role as leaders in organizations as follows: when we know what our purpose is, we know *why* we put ourselves through the hard work of bringing a particular *what* to life. The stronger the *why*, the more we are willing to apply ourselves fully to execute a difficult *how*, to realize our *what*. This valuable realization unites leaders and their followers and turns them into a powerful force. So purpose is, therefore, about how as leaders we align with our company and team members, and harness the power of our vision and purpose to execute our aims and goals. I'm going to start by looking at substantial research on purpose so that you can see the impact it's had on corporations around the world, and then we'll go on to look at how you can use this research both for your own evolution as a leader and for the growth of your team, so that you too can powerfully align with and operate from this place.

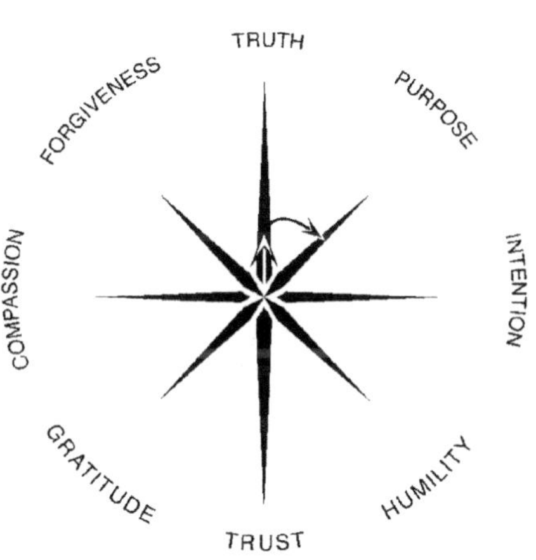

CORPORATE RESEARCH ON PURPOSE AND MEANING

For the last 10 years or so there has been a push for purpose, which can be seen in many leading organizations around the world. If we look at why this push came about, we see that the Baby Boomer generation sacrificed a lot of their joy for hard work, and for the safety of their children. Generation X then copied the behavior of their parent Boomers and worked equally hard for record high levels of material gain and quality of life. There was a tendency to stay in careers for a lifetime, regardless of satisfaction levels. The generation of children who grew up watching the sacrifices of both Boomers and Generation X revolted against this pattern, and began to ask for something more. For those coming after, a lot of elements that were paramount for the Boomers and Xers don't have the same value anymore. Friends and travel have a higher status for the younger generations than wealth and accumulation, and organizations that have a higher purpose that people can truly aspire to are more popular than ever. In short, there is a greater appeal for the younger generations to do something that matters. The need to do something that matters seems to also be fueled by the various crises that humanity is dealing with, such as polluted air and oceans, rising temperatures, melting glaciers, as well as a whole host of socio-political and economical injustices. Many prefer to work for companies that have bypassed surface values: they are calling us into something deeper because they *speak the language of the soul.* They make us feel that we'll be spending our lives doing something meaningful and that in the end we will have mattered. Being here for some other reason than making money so that we can live and buy things—*this* is what is really calling people forward in these current times.

The creation of a purposeful workplace impacts both employers and employees simultaneously. When our employees feel a sense of purpose, and that their purpose is acknowledged and nurtured, they show up differently in the workplace too. There is a growing body of research proving that a strong sense of purpose can provide sustained discretionary effort that goes way beyond the normal mandatory effort in the workplace. In his book *Drive,* Daniel Pink makes a compelling argument for additional drive that stems not only from increased financial compensation, but from three key elements: purpose, mastery and autonomy. In other words, "Help me understand *why* this is important, help me to constantly *get better at it,* and *trust me with the space and freedom to work.*"

Some organizations have carried out interesting and impactful studies into the power of purpose. KPMG, a global audit, tax and financial advisory service, conducted a comprehensive project among their employees, which they called the Higher Purpose Initiative.[1] It followed an annual employee survey, which revealed one item as a particularly strong driver of employee engagement, retention, and pride: "I feel like my job has special meaning and is not just a job." In their initiative, KPMG encouraged their employees to talk about and demonstrate what they felt was meaningful about their jobs. From there, they helped each employee create a purpose statement poster: a visual representation of what they do condensed into a single statement that summarized each individual's purpose in the company.

The firm set out to collect at least 10,000 stories and ended up with more than 40,000 from their 29,000 employees. Across the board, what this initiative uncovered is that whatever their job, the evidence is overwhelming that people want to lead a meaningful life.

Meaning and purpose can be a guiding force, not only for individual employees, but for the whole company too. If we take a look at Google, we realize that their mission is "to organize the world's information and make it universally accessible and useful." The founders Larry Page and Sergey Brin had a vision which was guided by this purpose, and it sits at the heart of everything they do.

Particularly when a company's purpose is based on values that align with the evolution of our planet, and they tackle some of humanity's core issues, they experience greater employee satisfaction and retention. An extensive survey carried out by Net Impact in collaboration with Rutgers University shows that employees who say they have the opportunity to make a direct social and environmental impact through their work report higher satisfaction levels than those who don't. In fact, employees who say they can make an impact while on the job, report greater satisfaction than those who can't by a staggering 2:1 ratio. In other words, people are twice as likely to be satisfied if their work means something to them, and is aligned to the greater good.

We can, therefore, see that purpose is integral to every element of your company or corporation. But like every aspect of the Inner Compass, purpose needs to start with you.

DEFINING PURPOSE

In my early days of business consultancy, I was a soft skills trainer. One of my offerings was a seminar on setting goals. Like many overachievers, I would lock myself away, prioritizing those goals, constantly refining them and finding ways to achieve them. I had won awards, started a business in a foreign country, and won some important clients, which was what my goals were focused on. Yet 10 years in, I was divorced, emotionally depleted, and teetering on the edge of bankruptcy.

I realized that yes, I had goals, but they were ego-driven goals built on false premises. In other words, they were mechanical goals built on *outer* achievements, with little or no connection to my *inner* reality. I made them with my head completely divorced from my heart, and as result I had lost my marriage, my connection to myself and was taking risks and pushing all limits, without really knowing why.

Contrast this with where I am today: when I carry out the Inner Compass work with myself and I talk about achieving something, I never set a goal without connecting it to my core. This part of the Compass is about what's meaningful to me and the use of my time on this earth. We can think about purpose in terms of:

1. What I'm passionate about and what I love doing.
2. Ideally I should be good at it.
3. I can get paid for it and earn a living with it.
4. It's something the world needs.

What's meaningful is different for everyone, and on a global level, many non-Western cultures have words for purpose that are deeper than the ones we use in the West. In Japan, they use the term Ikigai: one word for meaningfulness in life.

In Persian culture, there is a similar concept in the word Arman. Mammad, an Iranian associate of mine, describes Arman as "The fire that sits at the center of everything you do." He shared, "You can't fake your Arman, and it's different from the Western concept of purpose, which seems to be based on goals and dreams. For Iranians, Arman is much more closely linked to living a life of truth and fulfilling our purpose without denying that truth." Mammad built a highly successful US-based international tech conference company, but he left it behind when he realized it was not his Arman. "Living in New York during the Trump era, and being faced with the discomfort and misalignment of that period, my awareness of socio-economic inequality became such a guiding force that my real Arman (which was more aligned with my soul) was brought forth," he said. He walked away from his conference company, and spent a year agonizing over his next move before founding a New York-based non-profit organization that tackled food insecurity, and working on a cryptocurrency project for social good. "That year of agonizing about my next move was extremely uncomfortable," he shared, "and there was much doubt and confusion along the way. But finding your Arman is not always going to be comfortable, straightforward and easy. Sometimes you need to really be willing to suffer to be truthful to yourself."

In his book *A New Earth*, spiritual teacher Eckhart Tolle defines both inner and outer purpose—having an inner alignment with who I am in the present moment and how that alignment manifests in the outer world. My inner purpose is learning to be my true self in any given moment and recognizing that there are many layers to that truth. I will probably never finish that alignment work in my lifetime; it's ongoing and it's a curiosity that sits in the center of everything I do. My outer purpose is to inspire others to do the same, and the field I have chosen to do that in is the corporate world.

And for everyone this is different. I was on a retreat many years ago and we were defining our purpose when one woman said, "My purpose is to be." At the time I felt the sentence was incomplete, and that she didn't get it; but later I realized that she just wanted to be the purest form of herself. So there is no right or wrong answer on what your purpose is. It's deeply personal and what's meaningful to you—but there is one fundamental element: it has to be something you can build your life upon.

Over the past decade, I've been working with a number of coaching exercises that my team and I use in succession on both our retreats and in-person coaching sessions. They are designed to take your focus away from the more Westernized aspects of purpose (which usually focus on material outcomes and the drive to achieve more), and center on what is most important to you.

PRACTICAL EXERCISES TO DEFINE WHAT IS MEANINGFUL TO YOU

When I started working with the Inner Compass, I was initially surprised by the number of people I coached who hadn't spent a moment on thinking about their purpose. Over time, I developed exercises and today, if you were on my retreat or working with me in person, we'd carry out a number of these exercises to support you to develop your purpose. Some of them are quick-fire exercises that you do without much thought, and others require deep contemplation.

In the previous chapter we started to unpack the truth of who you are. You likely began to see that what you thought was your truth was actually a story you were telling yourself. You identified with that story to the point where it became your persona, and you developed various character traits that served you on some level, but were not based on your most authentic truth. You started to peel away the ego layers and get to the core, and work out what was no longer relevant to you. Once we start to clear the ego patterns and get to the core of your truth, we can really get to work on what's driving you. Initially it's not necessarily about finding one single purpose, but rather a cluster of themes so we can see what's guiding you (and—as I highlight on my Inner Compass

Retreats—finding a cluster of themes is often less daunting to the ego than discovering one single purpose). You can work through the following four exercises to start to get to the heart of that truth.

(I) VALUES EXERCISE

We start with a values exercise and you are going to need a stopwatch for this one. It's going to help you get clearer on the values that are important to you. The stopwatch will help you carry this one out in the way that we do on my retreat. Set your stopwatch for 60 seconds and in that time pick six values from the list below that are important to you (and if there is a value that is missing below, you can also add your own):

Accomplishment	Communication	Fun	Partnership
Achievement	Community	Health	Power
Adventure	Competency	Humor	Privacy
Altruism	Connection	Integrity	Professionalism
Authenticity	Creativity	Intimacy	Reputation
Autonomy	Curiosity	Joy	Respect
Balance	Excellence	Justice	Security
Clarity	Family	Loyalty	Self-Care
Collaboration	Flexibility	Openness	Self-Mastery
Commitment	Friendship	Orderliness	Service
Conscientiousness	Fulfillment	Personal Growth	Spirituality

Now set your watch for another 30 seconds. Take two out of your list that seem to you less important so you only have four left.

Again, set your watch for another 30 seconds, and take a further two out so you are just left with two. What this exercise does is bypass the mind so that you can get to the heart of what is really important to you. Now that you are left with two, take a moment to make a note about why these two are your guiding force.

It's essential to take some time to really think about why these values are your guiding force and to write this down. In many cases, there will be a kind of surface answer. You might find yourself breezing over your questions and giving an answer off the top of your head, but on deeper reflection you realize that it's a surface answer or an ego-based answer, and there is something else underneath. This happened to me back when I was in my early thirties and I went to a seminar where I was asked to pick the values that were important to me. When I went home I proudly showed my wife (at that time) my list of core values and she immediately noticed that family was at the top of my list. Her response was, "Really? How can that be when we don't see you." So why did I have family at the top of my list back then even though it wasn't true? It's because it was what was expected of me and how I wanted others to perceive me, rather than what was real for me at that time. But in hindsight, I believe that between the years of 27-38 my ego overpowered those true values that I held inside. I wanted to be seen as someone who was successful in my job. And I worked around the clock to prove that. Underneath that drive, biding its time to take on a more meaningful role in my life, was the value of growth, or removing the layers of who I was to be the truest version of myself. As this process took time, my family did not receive much of my attention and energy then. So it's essential not to pick what's expected or the first thing that comes to mind, but rather, what is real to you as you carefully look at the roles you have been playing.

And in an aside, these days, the value of family is actually paramount to me. My wife Svava and I built a retreat center together, and the time we spend there with our children (who actively helped us build it) are among my most treasured moments in life.

(II) PURPOSE QUESTIONS

I sometimes joke that the meaning of life can't be tackled in a seminar or even in a book. Yet we are tackling it anyway! We need to not only touch on these questions, but consider them deeply for our Inner Compass work. We are carrying out this four-part process because we are really getting to the core of what is important and meaningful to you. Next, consider the following (and while the previous exercise was quick-fire, this one is designed so that you can take your time to consider what is really meaningful to you):

1. What's my purpose for being in a management role?
2. What do I find meaningful in that?
3. If people had free choice, why should anyone want to follow me as their leader?

4. If there is a higher purpose in my leadership of people, what would it be?
5. Besides helping my team to reach company goals, what values do I deliver to them?
6. If I want to lead a meaningful life, what would that mean?
7. If I look at everything in my life, what do I value most, and what is most meaningful to me?
8. How much of my time is spent on the things that are meaningful?
9. In the end, what do I want to be remembered for?
10. If money was no longer a motivator for me, what would I do with the rest of my life?

Now take a moment to consider to what extent your answers are playing out in reality. If your purpose is kids and family but—like me in the past—you work 70 hours a week, then if you want to live authentically, you are probably going to want to take a look at that. You are also going to likely be aware of any resistance this brings up in you. When you start digging into the truth about who you are and you find something meaningful, you may realize that yes, you do see that you could lead a more purposeful life. But if that's not how you have led your life up until now, why should the whole setup of your life fit that newly-found purpose? And if it doesn't fit, are you ready to work on rearranging it so it does? For some people that I've coached, this can be a cause of stress and anxiety, especially when they have neglected this area and they are suddenly being called to look at it. The other side of that is that you are being called to evolve as a leader. And some of that is becoming aware of the parts of you that are asking to grow. Aligning yourself with purpose is often the spark that lights the fuel for the rest of your growth journey, and often it will spark a 180-degree turn. For example, I've had people quit their jobs, and go and find work in a different organization. I've had others who stay in the same organization, but in a different role.

I'm reminded of a CEO of a financial services company who, as we worked together, admitted that he did not find much purpose in the actual products and services his business offered, but he did find it in shaping the culture of the workplace. His aim was to create a culture guided by moral leadership, where people could fearlessly reveal their talents and be the best version of themselves. He stayed in that role even when offered a bigger CEO role elsewhere. I'm also thinking of a bank executive who had minimum exposure to the Inner Compass, but was strongly triggered by the purpose questions above. She went on to use her management expertise to take on an influential role in a charitable organization helping people in need on the African continent. And I remember a woman who was a manager at a global sporting goods company who—after long conversations with her spouse—decided to walk away from a well-paid job to become a coach. She truly flourishes in the role and feels she is making a valuable contribution in every coaching conversation.

(III) MEANINGFUL FLOW

When you have built purpose into your life, you are more able to stay in "meaningful flow." To get there, consider working with these four questions:

1. What do I love to do in my life?
2. What am I very good at?
3. What does the world need?
4. Can I earn a living by doing something that I am good at, that I love doing and the world needs?

Choose a partner to work with that you trust, and ease into a light, meditative state, where your mind is relaxed. Your partner asks you the first question. Staying in this meditative state, you speak what comes to you. Your partner documents or records your answers. Without any sense of rush, your partner moves you from question to question, and the only thing you focus on is listening to your inner self. (It's essential to avoid cognitive thinking in this process.) Where all 4 answers meet in the middle, you will find a meaningful overlap that represents purposeful work for you. And it is in this place that you want to be living, breathing and moving. If you are able to operate from this place, you will experience a significant increase in moments of "meaningful flow" in your life.

You may notice that one of the core aspects of finding this meaningful flow is ensuring that you focus on something that the world needs. This is perhaps where purpose in the Inner Compass differs from much of the purpose work that you will see in Western "pop spirituality" and self-help. There has been a trend over this past decade in popular spirituality to find our purpose. However, this trend has often been very one-sided. It's been focused on doing what you love, without much connection to whether what you love doing is something that the world also needs. The Inner Compass balances this so that it's a combination of what you are being called to do, and how that is useful to the wider world as well.

(IV) REFLECTION EXERCISE

We round out this practical section with a powerful reflection exercise. Imagine you are a fly on the wall at your 70th birthday party. Who is there? How are you feeling physically, mentally and emotionally? What is your life situation, and when you look back on your life, what was meaningful and what were you proud of that allows you to say you led a purposeful life?

DOES YOUR ORGANIZATION ALIGN WITH YOUR PURPOSE?

Now that we've done some focused exploratory work to find out your true purpose, there is one more core consideration that is crucial for you as a leader. *If you want to live your purpose and you are in a management role, it would make sense that you work for an organization that is a good platform for your purpose.* Your organization needs to do one of two things: either (i) have a purpose similar to yours, or (ii) show understanding of the purpose you have chosen.

REFLECTION POINT: If you are a manager who enjoys seeing people grow and realizing their potential, but you work for an organization where you are not given the space or time to work on this topic, and receive no support for it, or you are met with limited understanding of it, why would you stay? (Because if we sacrifice purpose for a temporary feeling of comfort and safety, we should be aware that we are sacrificing long-term fulfillment in life.) Why not find an organization that enables your purpose of empowering others? Once you understand your cluster of themes, are you in the right place? What if your time could be spent on purposeful stuff? If you find a company where you are a manager and their purpose and yours are aligned, what about the rest of the people on your team? Are they also aligned?

Let's say you have defined your purpose in life to be: "Stability and security for my family." Then you would want to look for a workplace that embodies exactly those values. This way the workplace becomes a harmonious platform for your purpose. If, on the other hand, you have defined your purpose in life as "Expanding everyone's awareness of our planet's fragile ecosystem," and your current company doesn't reflect these values, a different type of workplace might be a better fit for you.

Where a leader's vision and purpose are clearly aligned with those of the organization, energetic momentum is created. Put simply, people feel they are doing meaningful work. This type of energy explains why people in smaller start-ups often report having fun at work and seemingly endless energy, while at the same time working insane hours. As I write this, I'm thinking of the Icelandic power company that I've been working with. In Iceland, we almost only have green energy and it means we are a source of inspiration for other countries around the world. The money that this power company generates also reduces our taxes. Everyone I speak to at that company feels inspired by the role that they play. It generates as much revenue for Icelandic society as the fishing industry, yet only 300 people run that business. Everybody that works there feels a sense of pride to be contributing to their country in that way, and a sense of purpose built on their passion for sharing green energy.

There is also a famous example of this kind of united passion when workers at the BMW mini-plant in Oxford, UK, were fighting to save their plant. Geographically, the fact that the plant was based in Oxford made little sense at all. Many of the workers had to drive 90 mins for minimum to moderate pay. Oxford is one of the most expensive cities in the UK, so keeping the plant there was almost nonsensical. But the fight was about protecting jobs and it was carried out by people who had the best intentions for themselves and their families. Around 400 managers harnessed their own passion to become more collaborative, solution-oriented and they made it one of the best performing ones in the industry. (This was announced by *JD Power*, a leading magazine in the automotive industry.) So we see, once again, a company united by purpose and the outcomes that it brings.

WHEN YOUR ORGANIZATION ISN'T INTERESTED IN YOUR PURPOSE

So far we've been focusing on all the positive attributes of purpose, but I also want to acknowledge that this topic is not always welcomed by organizations.

It is difficult for someone with a clear purpose to work in an organization and team that have no purpose. It is also difficult for organizations to have a meaningful purpose as their guiding light if teams or individuals within that company do not connect with a united sense of purpose. In terms of making the Inner Compass something for leaders to work with, we have to take the view that it begins with us personally. You work with your team and together you actively support the purpose of the organization you work for. Ideally you need a CEO who works with you on a purpose statement that cascades down through the company.

If the core elements of your purpose aren't met by the company you work for and you have committed to an authentic Inner Compass journey, it might be time to reassess. You can probably already imagine how frustrating it would be if you spent all your time creating a clear purpose and then nobody else in your company was interested. I had a similar experience with a brand that I work with, where the CEO wants purpose stricken from the leadership program. He feels it has been overused, doesn't see the value of it and believes that it has been detracting from short-term profit focus. This development has been incredibly demoralizing for his employees who have been working on increasing a deeper sense of meaningfulness for themselves and their colleagues. Many feel they are being asked to snap back to a more "old school" way of working. They have been seeking ways to lead from beyond ego and subsequently believe that they are being asked to go back to a way of working that is more ego-driven.

It takes courage to assess where your organization is and whether it is a match for you. The idea of aligning with purpose is to give yourself and the organization you choose to work for full access to your intrinsic motivation, along with all the creativity and resilience this brings. This offers a completely different path than picking an industry that simply pays well, or a company that happens to offer you a job. You need to aim for a career that taps into the real you. That deeper part of yourself that knows what meaningful impact it wants to make. *Then* you can move forward with your purpose at the heart of everything you do. If your current company can't offer you this, it might be time to take stock.

Now that we have defined a clearly set and meaningful purpose, the next step with your Inner Compass work is to discover how ego often derails purpose, and how to operate with intention and develop humility, so that you can stay on track with your vision.

SECOND SEGMENT
MEETING THE EGO

PART 3

CHAPTER 4 INTENTION

I don't have any control over what actually happens, except for that I have full control over my will for myself, my intention and why I'm there. **SZA**

If purpose is the fire of the Inner Compass, then intention is the will to keep fueling that fire. It's the conscious act of keeping that fire burning, despite the challenges you encounter. When you have become clear on your truth and established your leadership purpose, the question then becomes "How am I going to ensure that I live my life and lead my team with my true purpose at the forefront?" The answer to that question lies in the way you set a clear, unwavering intention so that you actually show up in life as the person you are becoming inside.

Every cause has an effect, and intention is the driving force behind that cause. It ensures that our "why" goes into action. And even when we are not aware of our intention, our cause creates an effect. But with the Inner Compass, we create a *conscious intention*, which is rooted in purpose, and *this becomes a guiding force for everything we do*. When we set a clear and focused intention that is based on our purpose, we steer our course with a completely different quality than when we take action without an intention in mind. Here are three questions you can ask yourself : "What is my intention right now?" "What is my purpose right now?" "Can I shift and take a step towards it in this moment?" and to imagine where your life would be in three years' time if you dedicated yourself to living intentionally in any given moment.

There is, however, a challenge with living intentionally, and that challenge is the ego. Our ego derails our intention, not because it is working against us, but because it's part of a protective layer that is working to keep us safe. It takes us out of the present moment and into an instinctual story: a story about how we need to be focused on surviving imminent threats, rather than taking the high road to a purposeful life. *Most of us are torn between the instinct to survive and an inner calling to create something more meaningful.* If unchecked, the ego can pull us back to our familiar safety patterns, derailing our intentionality in the process.

We also don't just jump straight into intentionality: many people fall short if they do. If you start trying to set an intention without getting to your truth and clarifying your purpose, your ego will pull you back at the first hurdle and your intention will lack substance and depth. Most of us overestimate what we can achieve in the short term and underestimate what we can achieve in the long term. We need a healthy relationship with our truth and a clearly-defined purpose so that we can set the course with our intention and stay powerfully on track with a realistic vision.

So in this chapter, we'll look at how to set a powerful intention, grounded in our truth and purpose, and how to stay true to that intention when our ego tries to derail us. We'll see how intentionality—when set correctly—can be a powerful flame that keeps your purpose alight, and how you can consciously course correct so you keep that intention at the forefront of your actions.

HOW YOUR PRESENCE AS A LEADER IS REFLECTED IN YOUR INTENTION

So far in your Inner Compass journey you have combined the *truth* of who you are, with the *purpose* of your contribution. Now we are manifesting those two elements in a meaningful way through the power of your *intention*.

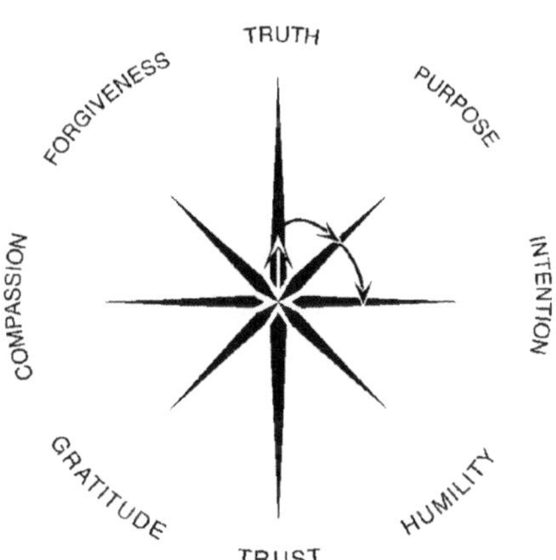

If you take the first element of the Compass—truth—it's about digging into who you truly are. As you peel away the fear-based layers, you get closer to your core, and start to ask "What is meaningful and purposeful to my core?" Once you discover your purpose, the next step is to clarify your intention. But there is a thread that runs through it all. The majority of your time needs to be spent in the present, and on the question "Who am I now?" Intention is in the now. As a leader, this means being present to who you are in *this* moment.

Purpose and intention can't be a package that you aim to reach 15 years from now. The past and the future don't exist. We only have today. We only have now. This moment. As leaders, as managers, as human beings, in every moment we need to ask, "What is the purpose for me now?" Not in five years, not in 10 years. Now. "What is my purpose in this moment?" And this becomes your guiding force.

Personally, when I was figuring out my purpose to be the truest version of myself and to be connected to my inner core, I realized that it wouldn't work to be the truest version of myself in the future. It had to be now, in this moment. I had to learn to live from that place. And that really is why presence plays such a big role in intention (and in every other element of the Inner Compass). It's a practice for every moment, rather than setting a one-time intention and then putting it aside until the next self-assessment.

The reality is that most of us have had the experience of reading a good book, have attended a leadership development program or engaged in some other activity that inspired us to be more purposeful and intentional, and at that time, all we wanted to do was to bring that vision to life. However, once we got back to the office, the inspiration faded, we got back to our old habits and our good intentions vanished. Quite often, we fall short of making those changes because we don't remain present with them, or practice applying them consciously and with intentionality in each moment.

GIVING FULL ATTENTION TO OUR INTENTION

When we think about *intention*, we actually need to start with *attention*. The most precious thing we have in our lives is our attention. A friend of mine, Gudni Gunnarsson—who is an Icelandic spiritual teacher—once said, "Everything you give your attention to grows and flourishes. Everything you deny your attention withers and dies."

In the last chapter, we started to look at your purpose, and to ask how much of your attention was actually on that purpose. If you are a parent and you put most of your attention on your child, then it's likely that you will develop a closer relationship with your child, but your career won't necessarily flourish. Another parent might put all their attention on their career, but find themselves with estranged children. It is the attention, then, that we place on any given area of our life that will cause that area to grow.

So living an intentional life is about where you choose to place your attention in this moment. If we take this into your role as a leader, imagine if you go into a performance appraisal meeting but you are not actually there, mentally. You might be distracted by the conditions of the bonus scheme. You might begin to imagine that if you praise your employee too highly, it's going to cost you money. Your distractions might include how other people perceive him. Perhaps there are two or three high profile leaders who don't rate his performance. So what's your intention at this time? To make sure you don't pay him more? To let those two or three high-ranking people influence you? Being distracted by these outside influences likely means that your full attention is not with your true intention for that employee.

When I asked one manager I coached what his intention was when he entered appraisals, and how he gave his attention to his employees, he answered: "My intention is to be 100 percent there with them. To be there with my people. If I focus on the agendas of others, if I think too hard about financial outcomes, I'm actually acting from the part of me that is afraid to make decisions that are true to my purpose and intention." The question is, are you willing to do the same? Are you resigned to living a life of fear, creating coping strategies so that you can get through your day, or do you want to break free and respond from a place of "I want to be present to this moment in a purposeful and meaningful way."

As a manager, I always do my best to be present for my team in this way too. A new employee recently said, "I don't know how you do it. I catch you in between meetings, and not only do I get your full attention, but

I sense your intention to help me solve the problem. How do you do that?" The truth is, I try to just be in the moment with my employees, giving them my full attention (and it's a practice that I am still constantly working on, rather than something that I am able to do 100 percent of the time). One of my passions is the fact that you can't live in the past even if it was only five minutes ago. And you can't live in the future either. Neither one of them exists. But what if this moment is the most powerful moment ever? That's how I endeavor to live and show up for my employees and in my daily life, and that involves giving them my full attention when I'm communicating with them. (I also want to say that this is not a practice that always comes easily to me. I used to always be one or two steps ahead in my mind. I lived in the future. And I still catch myself there, more often than I would like to admit! But there is definitely progress with this practice over time.)

If my intention is just to solve the problem, but I ruffle feathers or make people want to cry, then all the attention is on solving the problem, but that has a potential cost to my team members. If I stay in problem-solving mode without connecting to my team, over the long term that habit would be destructive and might cause collateral damage. They'd start to become cautious of me. They wouldn't offer to take risks. They would start to stay in their corner, and not look across at other areas to solve problems themselves. And if I do this consistently, the word would start to spread. This is the cost of solving the problem without intentionality. Instead, if I ask myself, "Why am I here, what is expected of me, what is my purpose and intention, and how does that help the problem we are here to fix?" it changes the way I show up. And again, I wouldn't say I've mastered this, but my attention is always on this approach.

Similarly, when I meet with people—either within my company or those from outside—I think: "What is the purpose of attending this meeting? Is it in alignment with my inner purpose?" And when you connect with your inner purpose and get present with it, you show up in a semi-meditative state, and there is this kind of energy field you can sense. All this is not something that is easy to put into words for most of us, yet we know how draining it is to be distracted, and how different it feels to show up fully.

AWARENESS EXERCISE: Before the start of each call (or meeting), ask yourself, "Why am I doing this call (or meeting)? What is my intention?" Notice how your focus changes when you enter with clear intentionality.

TRUE INTENTION

One member of my team was coaching a manager who complained that when he asked for feedback, he didn't get any replies. The coach asked, "If they had given it to you, what would you have done with it?" The manager admitted that he wouldn't have done anything with it. "These are crazy times. I'm just trying to survive each week. I'm overworked. In the middle of all that, I attended a seminar where they advised us to ask for feedback, so that's exactly what I did." So the coach asked: "What did your team read into it?" He replied, "Probably that there was actually no true intent." People sense true intention. In his case it was mechanical. And his team responded accordingly. So when we look at intention, we need to be sure that it is true intention, and not just a mechanical response based on what we think we should do. Before we progress any further, we can take a moment to reflect on just how much true intention is currently driving you.

TRUE INTENTION QUESTIONS

Here are some questions to help you go deeper:

- As a person or as a leader, to what degree are you currently getting the effect you hoped for at work?
- If you are getting this effect, what core intention is driving it?
- If you are not, what purpose-driven intention is missing?
- Is it part of your sincere intention to develop your team further?
- In which way would that work help you live your purpose?
- In which way does your work on developing your team help each of them to live their purpose?

HOW INTENTION RELATES TO EGO

In the previous example where the manager asked for feedback from his team, we saw that he didn't receive it because he didn't set a true intention. You could say that an intention of this nature is ego-based because it's motivated by ticking boxes and how we want to be perceived rather than being intentional. But there is also a much more fundamental component to how intention relates to ego and how ego can derail intention if we are not operating from awareness.

If you think back to our earlier chapters on consciousness and truth, we started to look at how our ego patterns form as protective mechanisms in response to our life experiences. We looked specifically at how fear can keep us from operating consciously. Fear is a huge topic in Inner Compass leadership and we come back to it time and time again—and it shows up very specifically when it comes to setting intentions. If your purpose has its roots based in fear, it reinforces your ego patterns, and particularly if your ego is strong, it will feel threatened by an additional meaningful purpose and intention.

Real purpose comes from your *inner* self. That's why it is called the Inner Compass. It comes from the part that was always there before fear created protective layers. If you come from that place, you cannot be operating from fear. In the chapter on purpose, we talked about what is meaningful to you. And if you ask yourself the question "What is meaningful for me?" and all your ego layers are still in place and you haven't explored your inner self, you will very quickly come up against a major challenge. So, for example, you might have financial and physical security as your purpose. You get a good job and keep it, and are reasonably satisfied for a while, but this is just the surface, and your ego keeps you right there. We have to get beyond the ego and find our true purpose to live intentionally.

HOW THE SURVIVAL MODE RELATES TO INTENTION

There is a company that one of my team works with and the senior management has a consistent fear-based attitude of "What if something goes wrong?" As was highlighted previously, when we operate from survival-based fears, we will never be able to do our best work, because the higher centers of our brain related to creativity and consciousness shut down in favor of ensuring that we survive.

Our survival response is what keeps us alive. Even though it can feel like it is against us at times, it can help to remember that it is a programmed response based on the experiences that have gone before. It comes from strategies that we learned when we were younger that kept us safe, which become subconscious patterns which are usually outdated. Even if we've lived a life based on survival, almost all of us have had moments where we get that sense or feeling that there is something more to life. This is the inner calling that has been part of our evolution as a human species.

So there are these two elements existing within us all the time: the one that is fighting for our survival and the one that is working towards our expansion and evolution. As leaders we need to set an intention to focus our energy on the part of us that is becoming more conscious. This means being aware of, and being able to meet ourselves in, the part of us that may get triggered into survival. We are breaking down the roles, for ourselves internally and for those we lead.

We all fall into a trap of some kind. A certain percentage of our days will be spent in the urge to survive. And a certain percentage will be spent trusting, being open, curious and learning. When you understand that you have a choice, the question becomes: "How much of my life do I want to spend in fear, and how much do I want to spend in expansion and curiosity?" And if you choose the latter, it's then a matter of breaking down the conditioning of fear based on all that you have experienced. This includes the general context in which you were raised—for example, you had a strict, overbearing father. It also includes any specific traumatic experiences that you had which might have shaped your sense of safety, such as a specific bullying event at school. You look at these experiences—both the context of how you were raised and the specific content of individual incidents that shaped your life—and you start to see how these layers explain the behaviors that have nothing to do with your inner self. And then you start to challenge every single story you have about yourself on a moment-to-moment basis so that you can start to be free of those patterns and live beyond your ego.

And as leaders, we also have to be able to recognize when our team members are triggered into survival, and set the intention to be compassionate to this aspect of their humanity. We need to understand that if we, say, approach an employee for an appraisal, it might trigger them into survival fears around loss of money or status. We need to set an intention to be compassionate about our employees' fears and tendencies to operate from survival thinking.

In his book *Drive*, Daniel Pink explores what actually creates drive that is free of survival thinking. In his research, he discovered that first you need to "pay people enough to take the topic of money off the table." This means that until the payment is fair, the perceived lack of money is demotivating and more money is needed before drive can be increased.

Once payment is perceived to be fair, there are three factors that are essential to drive. These factors deliver a bigger impact on performance than additional money. They are:

1. **Autonomy - Am** I trusted to self-manage?
2. **Purpose - Is** my work meaningful?
3. **Mastery - Am** I getting better at what I am doing?

The problem is that most managers are either unaware of these three factors or do not know how to implement them. This lack of awareness is often coupled with an environment where ego wants to control everything so that it can survive, so we end up seeing the opposite of those three qualities:

1. There is no autonomy: instead there is lots of control. The lack of trust makes me feel that I am unable to breathe, let alone expand into who I really am.

2. Purpose is based on survival. My focus becomes performing to the expected standards and thereby staying safe. A deeper and more fulfilling meaning has been lost in the fight to survive.
3. There is also little mastery because, by definition, mastery requires experimenting with new ways and experimentation means that things could go wrong. They ask me to tick boxes and achieve goals, but there is never true mastery because my main focus lies solely on safely accomplishing tasks.

So we are working towards giving our employees autonomy, taking steps to discover if they find their work meaningful and purposeful, and creating opportunities for mastery within their work. One element of ensuring that we create opportunities for autonomy, for example, can be seen in the concept of the Waterline. The Waterline is the point where you can make decisions without asking anyone above you. It's the marker that we create for our employees. Below the Waterline we are trusting our employees to make the right decisions, and therefore they have autonomy in decision-making so that problems don't escalate upwards. An excellent example of the Waterline was set by a leading hotel corporation. They gave chambermaids a budget of up to $1000 per guest, to be used with discretion to solve complaints and guarantee customer satisfaction. The way the chambermaids dealt with those guests changed because of the autonomy that had been created. They were empowered to help the customers, and although they almost never used any of the budget, the way they showed up changed because of the trust that was placed in them. Contrast this scenario to a chambermaid who has to run every single financial decision past their manager—and the fear and stress this can create for employees—and you can see how using the Waterline creates more autonomy for employees. This allows them to be freely purposeful and intentional within the context that the Waterline marker provides them.

HOW INTENTIONS FADE IF THE EGO DERAILS THEM

A few years ago, Jenny was a team leader in a collection agency. She had always enjoyed working with people and typically spent a large portion of her day moving from one agent to the next to monitor their work and coach them on their performance. Jenny had started as a call-center agent, but had accepted two promotions within a time frame of 18 months. She was happy with the increased pay and the company car, but she had never really stopped to think about what her promotion would mean. Now her management position made her responsible for over 300 agents and her focus was mostly administrative. She found herself spending more and more time on planning and reporting, and felt locked away in her office.

During a session with her coach, Jenny became strongly aware of her inner purpose, which was centered around being present with life-long learning and growth. It also became clear to her that her outer manifestation of that purpose was to help others to learn and grow. As a result, she set the intention to optimize her time management to free up time for developmental work, and to block time for exploratory conversations with some of her key people.

Six months later, Jenny admitted to having made very little progress. Her intention had faded in the face of the fact that her demanding job seemed to offer no space for this type of work, and she felt exhausted from dealing with all the reporting, planning and day-to-day administrative tasks. Now she also felt that she had failed at leading a more intentional and purposeful life. With some help from an Inner Compass coach, she took a deeper look at the real reasons behind why her intention faded, and uncovered a deep-rooted fear of not being good enough. The thought of handing in a plan that was not fully thought through, or a report with a mistake in it, was causing her to significantly overinvest in administrative tasks. She felt that her perfectionism was the number one driver behind her promotions (although her boss said it was because she was so good with people) and that if she were to ease off on her standards, her standing in the organization would suffer.

In summary, Jenny's deep-rooted fear of not being good enough activated an ego-driven defense mechanism in her, which was to be so perfect that no one would think of criticizing her. This drive was so strong that even though her inner self wanted to make the most meaningful change to her job that she could imagine, her ego never even gave her a chance to try it out. It was too afraid of "failing."

This is the number one reason good, purposeful intentions fade and disappear with so many people. Our subtle but very present fear-driven self-protection mechanism does not want to change what it believes to be a tried and tested success formula. It does not give us the peace of mind and the mental flexibility to risk anything that might jeopardize the status quo. And because this mechanism has had years and years of establishing itself, during which time we were more or less unaware of our real purpose, it may well be stronger than our intention. We have to be willing to recognize these patterns within ourselves time and time again, so that our intention doesn't get lost in the trappings of our ego.

HOW INTENTION RELATES TO MANIFESTATION

Up until this point, we've talked a lot about how intention changes your internal world, and how it can transform your interactions with others. We also need to acknowledge that when we are intentional—particularly when that intention is rooted in truth and purpose—it changes the way that we operate with our outer world too. In short, we are more likely to attract and align with other people who are operating intentionally, and it can seem that the way we dance with life has a completely different quality than when we are living unintentionally. What I have just written may find echoes for you in the worlds of pop spirituality and self-help, where attraction of abundance and manifestations are spoken about with great frequency. I want to be cautious with my use of terminology here because much of that dialogue has been overused and become clichéd. Since Rhonda Byrne released the film *The Secret* in 2006, there have been countless seminars worldwide on abundance and manifestation, and they have been seen in all walks of life, including the corporate world. If you ever encountered this work, you will likely have noted that it is built around the notion that what you focus on and give your attention to will manifest in your reality.

How the Inner Compass work differs from this is that this vital element of intention is being aligned with truth and purpose. If we do, indeed, get to our truth and define our purpose before we set our intention, we likely find that the way opportunities show up in our world are very different than if we blunder through life unaware of being governed by our patterns, unclear about our purpose, and without a clearly defined intention. So much of what we are doing in this part of the Compass is lining you up with what is true and purposeful for you and helping you set your intention so that you create the greatest opportunity for success.

It can be helpful to think of the difference between your intentionality for your own inner growth journey and your intentionality for what you are manifesting in your outer world—both on a personal and professional level. In your inner world you may have an intention to change dietary habits, exercise habits, behaviors, reactions, etc. These are all intentions that are reasonably within your control. In your outer world, you may have an intention to attract new projects or partnerships, expand your corporation or get promoted. These are elements that you don't necessarily have direct control over. But in clearing the way by doing your inner work to transform the patterns of your ego, clarifying your purpose, and setting a clear intention, you give yourself the best opportunity to manifest these potential futures because you are aligning yourself with them. The following two exercises are designed to prompt you to work with your purpose-driven intention.

INTENTION EXERCISE ONE

Step 1 is to focus on creating something short-term, i.e. in the next 30 days. This could, for example, be something simple like smiling and saying good morning to your team every morning, or finding someone to praise every week and leaving a thank-you note on their desk. It could also be a change in diet, a new exercise regimen or more time with your family. The intention needs to be something that matters deeply to you, and it needs to be based on a deep sense of purpose.

Step 2 is to decide on something to manifest in the medium term, over the next one to three years. Now we are moving closer to creating a vision of something that want to manifest in our lives at a certain point in time, without having a clear road map in our heads. Whatever it is that we want to achieve, such as having a more functional team, a promotion, a certain business impact, and so on, describe it as vividly as possible, in the present tense, and using strong and powerful language. Again, be certain that whatever you are envisioning is based on a deep sense of purpose.

Make sure you are clear on the steps and actions for both of the above intentions, and look for any pitfalls or potential ego derailments that might prevent you from moving forward. What steps do you need to take to ensure that your intention remains in the present with these goals? How will you assess that presence of intention in your day-to-day reality?

INTENTION EXERCISE TWO

In this exercise, you will talk through your truth and purpose findings with someone you trust implicitly, such as a significant other, a close friend or a mentor. Ask them to listen actively *with their heart* for what they feel and ask necessary clarification questions, without commenting or suggesting ideas. You only want them to understand how you are purposefully aligning with the present, why this is important to you and what the desired outer manifestation of this is. You don't want feedback on whether they think your intention is possible.

Talking through all of this may take you anywhere between 15-45 minutes, so make sure both of you have set aside enough undisturbed time. At the end of your explanation, ask your listener the following questions.

"As you listened to me speak about my truth, purpose and intention, what did you sense or feel? Where was my passion the clearest to you?"

We are tapping into our collective emotional intelligence in this exercise, and working in close cooperation with a purposeful intention.

Now that we have begun to explore how purpose and intention are derailed by ego, in the next chapter we are going to add a new quality to work on: humility. We'll see how humility is an antidote to ego and how we can use it to overcome the fear-driven self-protection mechanism that subconsciously derails intention.

CHAPTER 5
HUMILITY

Humility is not thinking less of yourself. It is thinking of yourself less. **C.S. Lewis**

When I was 27, I worked as the head of sales for an Icelandic broadcasting company. As a younger manager, I was highly driven and dressed to kill, but under the surface, I was deeply insecure. Struggling to manage my team of 10, I was given a consultant to help me grow. I liked this consultant as a person and he contributed a lot to us becoming a functional team.

One day, after working together for about a year, he and I sat together in my office discussing what our next steps could be. As I sat with him, deep in discussion, my office manager stuck her head around the door, interrupting me with something that she felt was an important matter. I didn't see the importance, and I blurted out something angrily, humiliating her in the process. Her face went red and she instantly retreated from the room. Expecting to return to the conversation with my consultant, this time it was my turn to be embarrassed. "What did you just say?" my consultant asked, scolding me like a kid. For several minutes more, he berated me for my behavior. And although I don't remember everything he said that day, I'll never forget his closing words. "You need to learn that humility is a strength."

I was not immediately receptive to this lesson. In fact, instead of taking it on board, I acted defensively (a common trait of the ego), deciding there must be something wrong with him. "He's not dressed immaculately. Who is he to tell me what to do? I can't work with this loser." These were the thoughts that ran through my head, and I decided he was incompetent, and made the decision not to call on him anymore. But I couldn't escape his closing words. They haunted me to the point where I was unable to rest. I reached out for books on the topic of humility and began to learn more. I must admit that it took me seven years to call him and thank him for one of the most valuable lessons of my life, but what started that day was a lesson in humility that I now attempt to live in every moment to my core.

Humility is an antidote to ego. If purpose and intention can be derailed by ego, humility is a quality that ensures we don't go off course, or it allows us to course correct if we do go off track. In this chapter, we'll look at the role humility plays in your Inner Compass journey. We'll work on developing this essential quality of leadership so that it becomes a key way of showing up, and you'll see how this impacts you to your core.

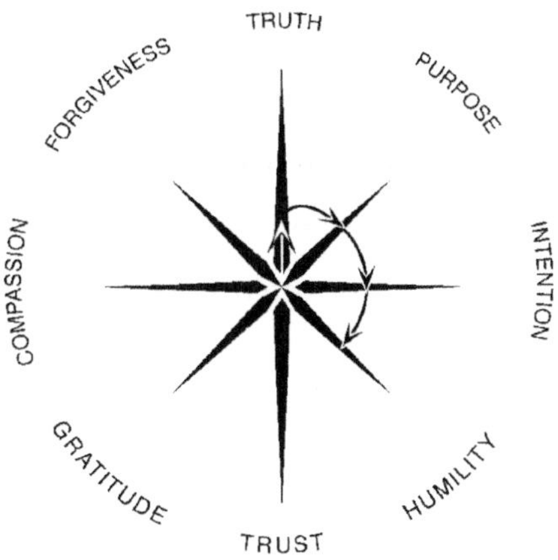

USING EASTERN PHILOSOPHY TO DEVELOP HUMILITY

Much of my journey with humility has come from asking myself the question "What is the strength in humility?" and exploring what my consultant meant that day when he shared that lesson with me. I sought answers from cultures all around the world, and one of the most powerful awakenings came from a business conference with a group of senior managers in China.

In Chinese business culture there is an understanding of the Eastern concept of yin and yang. The Western business world has favored the yang approach. Yang is characterized by boldness, strength and the ability to push forward. As Western business managers, this is ingrained in our psyche. During this particular conference, we had daily lessons from a Tai Chi master. He opened his demonstration by telling us, "It's interesting to me how you Western executives are all about yang. Instead of your usual mode of operation, I'm going to teach you how yin can be an even more powerful force." The Tai Chi master was short in stature but one of the most powerful presences I have encountered. The practice of Tai Chi is based on movements that were designed to evade force, and each movement is created so that, as your opponent comes towards you, you move in a way that keeps you stable and evades the attack, not through force, but through supple strength. And in that demonstration he also taught us about yin, and how it relates to humility.

To use the analogy of a cup, yang would be the clay you make a cup out of: it's something tangible and solid. Yin, on the other hand, is the empty space inside the cup, without which the cup would be useless. Just as we may overlook that empty space as a crucial part of the cup, so we tend to overlook humility as crucial to effective leadership. If you think about it, a lot of people have full cups, so they can't take on new knowledge. There is no space for new understandings and growth to come in, so they become stagnant, fixed and closed. Humility, on the other hand, is about openness. It's where we realize "I don't know all the answers or even all the questions. If I don't know everything, why should I pretend I do? I can be honest about my own limitations, and about what I know and don't know."

Honesty and openness come with humility. Your cup has space with this mental shift and you can take on more. You become a humble learner that others can approach with ideas, and you are constantly expanding because you understand that humility is the key to growth.

If you are open, honest and willing to learn, that is how you approach other people too. You are not bigger than they are, and you treat them with open curiosity and respect. You ask more questions than you give answers. You are willing to understand and learn. In Steven Covey's classic *The 7 Habits of Highly Successful People*, he shares that one of the keys to success is to seek first to understand and then to be understood. And this is where humility comes into play. We show up without the arrogance of thinking we are above others. When we listen, we are not just waiting to give our side of the story or dominate with our beliefs. We are open, honest, respectful and patient, and it transforms the way we communicate with others.

So if humility is yin and boldness is yang, it's easy to see how humility often gets overlooked in a Western business scenario. Yet that proactive pressure that comes with having to perform and be strong, if not coupled with humility, is what can lead us to dysfunctional teams, less human connection, less innovation and possibly physical exhaustion or burnout. We even project that onto our kids and this is where you see children with anxiety attacks under the pressure to perform. We forget to teach them the yin aspect of achieving (often because we haven't learned it ourselves). We forget to tell them "If you fail today, be kind and accepting of the situation. You can give it another shot tomorrow." And in doing so we create high performing achievers who don't know how to dance with the pressures of life because they are so focused on the outcome of winning. We do this to our children. And we do it to ourselves.

YOU CAN'T MEET YOUR EGO WITH FORCE

If we tie in what we know about yin and yang with the Inner Compass work, we understand that we can't meet ego with yang. In other words, we can't meet ego with force. You can't outsmart the ego because it's very cunning. You have to learn to disarm through surrender (which is something we'll be working through later on in this book), and humility is the way to ensure that ego isn't running the show.

My team and I often encounter yang CEOs who are not sure what to do with yin, so they try to reject this part of themselves. Yet one doesn't exist without the other. If you are someone who is new to embracing these yin elements, it can help if you look at the traditional yin and yang symbol. You'll see that the side that represents yin is black and the side that represents yang is white. However, you will see that there is also a spot of white on the yin side, and vice versa. These spots are there to remind us that everything is always in a constant state of flux. So instead of seeing ourselves as one or the other, we can see that we are both of these states, and each state contains an element of the other.

When I'm coaching individuals, particularly those who come across as more yang in nature, one of the things I'm doing is listening and waiting for a window of opportunity to be created. Humility gives us the options of waiting, listening and learning. It allows us to be more strategic as we take time to understand the situation better. One of the basic components of humility is patience. We are never going to jump into that patience 100 percent of the time if we are new to it. Instead, we are going to need to give it time to develop.

HOW TRUTH WORKS WITH HUMILITY

We've already talked about the essential nature of truth in the Inner Compass journey, and discussed how it's a starting point for anyone who is operating from a place of humility. When you find *the* truth for you in any given situation, it's like a boulder that cannot be moved. In chapter 3 we talked about Gandhi and how his purpose changed the plight of his nation. He gives us an example of what happens when we live the highest of truths. When you live with that kind of truth in your heart, the fact that you are alone with your opinion against everyone else's does not mean it's not true. That truth resonates through your entire being. It doesn't give you any peace until you vow to live by it and take actions that align with it. But this has to involve both your yang (which is the action) and your yin (which is your humility) in order for your truth to be a guiding force.

Without humility, truth can be a tricky area, particularly when the ego is strong. You'll see a religious cult leader who claims to have found their truth. They may have the purpose of creating a flock. They will prey on the vulnerable and manipulate the weak. Because they are without humility, they might have a strength or force, but something will be off. The true religious leader will be humble and their humility will be their guiding force.

WHAT A HUMBLE LEADER LOOKS LIKE

I've worked with Mike, a CEO of a financial services company in the UK, over a period of seven years. Mike embraced Inner Compass teachings in his life, and is a particularly humble leader.

Mike ran a very successful senior team in his financial services company, and then one day the company hired a head of finance. After assessing the way Mike's team worked, the new head of finance told him, "Something is off about this team. I don't see any Alpha males." "What if there aren't any?" Mike replied. The head of finance was confused. "How are you getting these exceptional results without them?" he asked. "I don't think you need Alpha pushiness to get great results," was Mike's response, and the impact of his team verified that. His team constantly ranked at or near the top of the metrics of the global organization they belonged to—a highly dynamic group whose energy you could describe as a healthy mix of yin and yang (although because this is so unusual in the corporate world, it's likely from the outside that they appeared more yin).

In the book *Good to Great,* Jim Collins talks about the special type of leadership that Mike embodied: humble on a personal level. This type of leader blends extreme personal humility with intense professional will. They combine personal humility but company boldness. If you asked a leader like this to express how they operate, they might tell you something along the lines of: "When it comes to the company, I will fight. When it comes to me, I stay humble." This kind of leader has flexibility and dynamism, and sways like a tree in the wind. For a leader of this nature, purpose and intention require boldness, but that boldness is *always* accompanied by humility so that yin and yang work together. When we reach this place in our Inner Compass journey, it can be described as the first heart opening. In fact, if you look at the Compass, humility and forgiveness are on the same axis and both of those qualities are more yin than yang.

We can see this in a recent example of global leadership by the former Chancellor of Germany, Angela Merkel, who said, *"Fear has never been a good adviser, neither in our personal lives, nor in our society."* Following her own Inner Compass, Merkel did not shy away from making difficult decisions. During the height of the Syrian refugee crisis, she had the moral courage to allow refugees to enter Germany. She did this because she felt it was the right thing to do for people in dire need, knowing full well that this could cost her her job as Chancellor. She followed her morals and took the higher road.

YOUR OWN DEVELOPMENT OF HUMILITY

Developing humility is definitely a process, particularly if your ego has been successfully leading the way for you. At this stage of your Inner Compass journey, you have begun to understand yourself, dug into your purpose and set a clear intention. This has required boldness, especially if you have allowed the fire to burn brightly when it's needed. But with this yang, you are also starting to develop the yin of humility.

For all of us who take this path, when we set out, we take first steps and we fall flat on our faces. And when we do, we bleed. That's where we need to be humble and turn up the humility even more. It's a learning process and each time you fall, you discover a bit more about yourself, and as you do, you trust yourself further and grow even more.

An Inner Compass leader humbly engages in the lifelong task of gaining self-knowledge and self-awareness. In their open-minded search, they find a meaningful purpose that they know is their North Star. And based on this knowledge, they set an unwavering intention to live their lives purposefully in the present moment. As they then go about manifesting this intention in their lives, they do not allow their fear-driven ego to derail their plans. They stay focused and determined to honor their truth, to live their purpose and stick to that intention. When their ego every now and then does wield its power, they embrace it with humility, recognizing their own frailty and then get back on track. The more they train their awareness, the quicker their ego moments subside. As a result, their teams know where they stand at all times and what they are taking a stand for. And if the teams feel aligned with this stand, they feel committed to their leader. This is how intention and humility together become a powerful foundation upon which to build a strong team.

HUMILITY EXERCISE

Think back to moments in time when someone or something was

pushing your hot buttons, and when your default reaction to that push was less than ideal. You know, one of those moments when you afterwards think, "Oh, I should have said ...." Or a moment when you think, "Oh, I should have kept my mouth shut." All of us have them from time to time, but their impact on our lives varies. As you record 2 or 3 of such incidents from the past, ask yourself what thoughts went through your mind back then, just before you reacted. What emotions accompanied those thoughts? Is it possible that this was in some way a fear-driven ego reaction to a perceived threat? (Remember that disrespect is also a form of threat, to which many of us display strong reactions.)

If your memory includes an afterthought similar to the ones mentioned above, you are basically saying that your reaction was less than ideal. And, you are saying that had you been given a bit more time and mental flexibility to think things through from a broader perspective, you might have reacted differently. Well, that extra time is available to you, if you can ease your ego's grip on those moments when you feel somehow threatened. So, to prepare for that, please finish the exercise by writing up how this situation you recalled might have developed differently, had you been able to embrace your ego with an attitude of humility. (Thereby instantaneously relaxing and freeing up your mind to see things from more perspectives.) What thoughts and emotions might have come to you in that state? What choices might have been available to you, through those resources?

HUMILITY IN ACTION

Once you start to get a clearer understanding of how your ego is derailing you, next you can start to develop your humility in everyday business scenarios. My team and I witnessed this happening with a manufacturing company we work with, when a recurring fault found in a metal part was causing significant loss of production volume and increasing production costs per unit. In a meeting between sister plants that both handle this part of the production process, managers' tempers were overheating and the discussion became counterproductive. It was one of a string of meetings that had taken place, and all of them had ended without resolution.

On this particular occasion, however, one of the managers—who is on an Inner Compass journey—was able to mentally step back and alter the course of the meeting. He calmly requested that the group take a pause for a moment before asking, "Gentlemen, if I am correct, all of us sitting in this room have gone through the Leadership Development Program of our plants, right?" To which they all agreed. He then added, "In that program we all learned about our own ego patterns and the ugly faces they can create. Is it possible that we are allowing our egos to run our discussions, rather than humbly listening to each other so that we can constructively solve this problem, without pointing the finger of blame?" His courage meant that the meeting continued in a completely different manner and the two teams made significant progress towards a sustainable solution. The manager who defused the situation showed how humility can be used effectively to disarm the ego in a group situation.

Now that we've taken time to consider how humility can derail the ego, in the next segment we'll look at how letting go of who you used to be and who you are telling yourself that you are will further evolve your journey with the Inner Compass. We'll be looking at developing trust—which will take on a completely different quality now that you have reached this stage of your Inner Compass work. We'll also get into forgiveness, so you can finally let go of any demons that are keeping you trapped in old ego patterns.

THIRD SEGMENT
LETTING GO

PART 3

CHAPTER 6
TRUST

As soon as you trust yourself, you will know how to live.
Johann Wolfgang von Goethe

You may have noticed others who are completely at ease about where they are heading in life. They will have the confidence to ask, "Is this right for me?" They do so, even if an opportunity might seem too good to miss. If the answer is no, they won't be living in fear of missing out. If they decide that their current job, or even career, isn't working for them, they find a way to move into something that is more aligned. Instead of operating from the fear that they won't be able to generate something equally great in the future, they are at peace with their choices and are able to let go. They are living in trust, and they radiate this peace with the track they are on. It's common that when others—even established and highly successful leaders—are exposed to this kind of leader, they feel an attraction to them and a sense that they are operating on a higher level. There is a sense of "How can they be so certain? They work hard, trust implicitly, make mistakes, forgive themselves easily and bounce back. I want some of what they have." And these are the kinds of qualities we are developing in you as a leader so that you will be able to operate in this way. Trust is the faith that drives this forward. You start to see signs that you are on the right path and you start to attract and align with others who have similar qualities.

If you want to be the kind of leader who lives in trust in this way, you need to do the groundwork first. In this chapter we'll look at how the previous elements of the Inner Compass come together to create a foundation on which trust is built.

THE GROUNDWORK THAT BRINGS TRUST TO LIFE

Trust is the faith that stabilizes the Inner Compass. For trust to sit right with the Compass, you need to have done the groundwork with the previous elements first. At this point, if you have been practically applying the work that we have been doing together, you have a much more thorough knowledge of yourself and greater understanding of your inner workings, your ego patterns and your core. You have found a purpose that is meaningful to you that you can build your life around. You have set a strong enough intention on how to manifest that purpose. You have understood the pitfalls and worked on being humble, and have

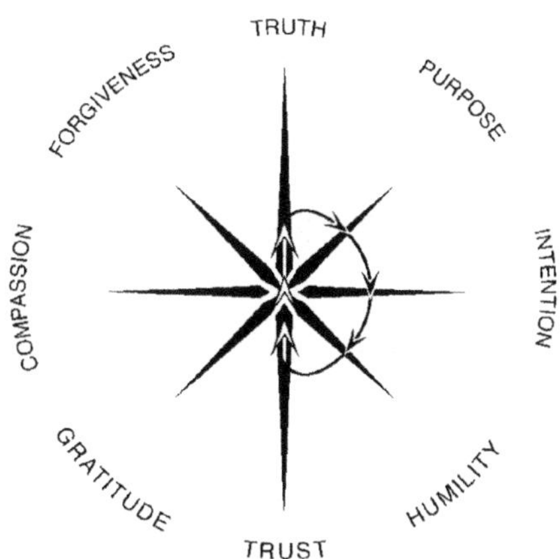

understood that humility helps you to harness your ego. When all these elements are combined, the next step is to follow your truth and stay true to your purpose of living your intention in the present. This is the stage where you let go of the need to control, surrendering into trust and realizing the personal freedom that comes when you aren't holding on to everything so tightly anymore.

At this stage, you are also on your way to recognizing when the ego is taking over, so you can continue to keep it in check. This is an ongoing process, and it can become a fascinating self-discovery, as you notice the familiar patterns of ego and feel a sense of strength in the moments that you no longer follow those patterns without a thought. As you take each step, you continually ask yourself, "Do I understand when I'm operating from ego and when I'm operating from my core?" You'll also be asking, "Am I able to recognize when subtle fear-based responses trigger me into survival thinking or fear-based action?" So, before you are able to trust implicitly, you have developed your sense of when you are operating from ego and when you are operating from your core. And when it comes to purpose, you have developed some trust in the authenticity of your intentions too. You'll know you're being triggered when you find yourself thinking thoughts along the lines of "If I have enough money to pay the debts, then I will be safe," or "I'm worried my team and I will not meet our targets by the end of the fiscal year." You start to recognize this kind of thinking as survival-based, and you ensure that these kinds of thoughts are not the ones running the show. At this stage, you start to develop an understanding that it all has to be more expansive than achieving team targets. You have garnered enough wisdom to set an intention that comes from your core, rather than an intention such as "I would like a new Jeep this year," and you steadfastly stick to that intention and notice the moment you go off course.

It's essential to remember that you will probably be making mistakes on the above process time and time again, and you need to give yourself room to consistently adapt to the growth you are inviting. It's good to remind yourself, particularly if you are a well-established and successful leader in a corporate environment, that you are there because you have already been willing to make mistakes and grow from them. Now, that willingness you have shown in your outer world needs to be taken inwards as you practice navigating your ego and fall many times in the process. Each time, you step into humility and say, "Let me have another look at myself." You refuse to give way to frustration when the ego takes over one more time. Once you get to trust, you will have been working on this for some time. If you are following your truth, and guided by your purpose, and you make intentional small steps every day doing the best you can, you start to trust that, whatever the outcome of that effort is, you are on the right track in life.

TRUSTING OTHERS

During the global pandemic, countless people were forced to work from home. Most managers did not know how to properly "manage" people and outcomes in this new paradigm, so people needed to be trusted to do their best under great distress. Many managers around the world were astounded to find that their team members could be trusted at this level!

We've already highlighted how this trust begins implicitly with you, but how does it manifest in your outer world so that others can be trusted too? This is where trust, faith and humility come together. If you believe that you are on a path where you are sending out all the signals that are relevant to your purpose, you can simultaneously make a silent agreement with yourself that everyone you meet on your path is your teacher too. This kind of thinking definitely needs a leap of faith from conventional wisdom, which is more focused on the sense that there are people above us, and people below us, and our aim in life is to always be the ones above, looking down. It levels the playing field for us to live in a more open-hearted way where we can either learn something from whoever crosses our path, or learn from what they show us about ourselves. There is a kind of freedom that comes from living this way. We move beyond our tendency to create an unconscious hierarchy where we judge someone to be above or below us, and we welcome every experience we have with others from this place.

I've seen how surrendering to this level of trust has impacted the evolution of my own company. In my early career, my life was strongly focused on being part of the Dale Carnegie Training organization, and one of my companies was Dale Carnegie, Germany, a successful venture which I sold in 2009. After that I worked solo with an assistant for over three years before hiring a young man who came straight from the conventional corporate world. I've never been a typical manager with an eye for detail, so we formed an alliance where initially, I won contracts and he became the general manager for the German leg of my business. I couldn't have built up the company so successfully without him, but we had different interests and approaches to conscious leadership, so eventually he went in a different direction. At this point, I took on board a different corporate person, who had spent three years on our advisory board, and this one was an accountant by trade who came at the perfect time. He was there for the start of the global pandemic and safely walked us through what we needed to do to secure our finances, doing an amazing job. His work gave us the financial confidence which enabled the company to concentrate on growth in the pandemic when others folded, and we were able to help our trainers navigate that difficult time financially as a result.

As time went on, it became apparent to me that to take our Inner Compass work forward, we at some point needed a manager who resonated strongly with the values that we were teaching, and who lived them to their core. Of particular importance were topics like trusting our team without micromanaging, being emotionally flexible and stable, and having a growth mindset that allows the questioning of all previous opinions and beliefs. I subsequently hired a female manager who embraced living from beyond ego. She is with us today, is very excited about the consciousness journey and is deeply committed to living and following the Compass.

When you look at the evolution of my Strategic Leadership company, particularly with the different management styles that have moved it forward, it's clear that everything has its time, and personally, I trusted the right person to be there for that time. I learned something from each one of these leaders—every single one of them was a valuable teacher—and I was open to the growth journey that came for me with the different styles and approaches.

I know for many corporate people this kind of trust can be really challenging. Often we've carved out a path by making everything "as it should be." We've been used to having a substantial level of control, and keeping many elements of our working relationships tightly contained. But if we are willing, we can evolve this approach so that each relationship brings its own lesson, and its own growth period. In order to do this, we need to be able to ask ourselves, "If I feel the need to control the outcome, which part of me is that?" Always, and without question, when I ask this in a coaching context, my client will answer something along the lines of "I see that it is the ego trying to keep me safe." Especially for leaders who have embraced the earlier elements of the Compass, when we get to trust, we already see where the ego is holding on. Your ego can always have a voice, but when it dominates you to the point where you don't trust anyone, before you know it you won't even trust yourself.

Essentially, what we are coming back to is a question I posed in chapter 3. Do you remember when we carried out the exercise of you being a fly on the wall of your 70th birthday celebration, and how you were reflecting on what it had felt like to live a purpose-driven life? The elements of trust we are discussing here are crucial because they allow your purpose to be lived out in combination with others around you. Do you trust yourself that you can lead a life that, when you look back, you can see that your time was spent purposefully and well? And once you have found a path to walk, do you trust that it is the right path for you?

When it comes to leading teams, all you can do is show them that you are truthful, that you purposefully live your intention, and that you are humble. In living by these Inner Compass qualities and modeling them to your team, you trust that it will, in turn, inspire them to be the best versions of themselves too. And it is on this foundation that you can guide and coach them. Throughout history, we've seen how modeling the highest qualities inspired others to do the same. There's a great example of this from the fact that Abraham Lincoln didn't run for president. He was active in the party, but the night before they were supposed to nominate the intended candidate, a scandal broke. At first the party couldn't agree on anyone. But then they all agreed on humble Abe. When elected, he formed his cabinet by including several members who thought they should have been president. His Minister of War was utterly convinced he himself should have been chosen, but Lincoln still chose him for his cabinet because he said he knew no one better for the job. He trusted people and he put his faith in them. By the time Lincoln was assassinated, that same Minister of War who initially believed he should have been president said, "Here lies the greatest of all of us." Lincoln simultaneously trusted people, and earned their trust from the humble behavior he modeled to them.

So, with the Inner Compass, trust boils down to: do I trust that this purpose is the right one for me? And when the answer is yes, you share your purpose with your team and see if they choose to walk the path with you. If they do, trust needs to be an implicit part of that path from day one. If any of your team members betray that trust, you will need to discuss it with them, because each of them basically becomes a partner on that path with you, and trust is what enables you to keep walking that path together.

HOW TRUST AND FAITH WORK TOGETHER

The year was 2006: the year that my life fell apart. I got a divorce, split from my business partner and almost went bankrupt. I felt that the whole way I believed life should be led had crumbled into pieces. I was stripped bare, and I'd spend my nights with my head buried in the pillow, tears streaming down my cheeks. Somewhere in the middle of my nightmare, I remembered that my grandmother's secret had always been to pray. I'm not someone who has ever been drawn to organized religion, but the way I prayed could more accurately be described as an act of faith, with the sense that there is something greater than our human existence. A lot of people ask me for strategies, and I could teach you strategies all day long (my company is called Strategic Leadership and it's built on the value of strategies), but the truth is that strategies mostly lack sustainability unless we have some kind of faith.

Within a few weeks of praying, I formed a new belief that although my life had seemingly disintegrated before my eyes, this was an opportunity to rebuild. My faith in something greater than the circumstances that I saw before me allowed me to rebuild something more meaningful and purposeful. If you think about it, you likely picked up this book because you had an initial urge to begin searching for a deeper truth than the one you were living. Even if your life was not falling apart like mine was at that time, something was calling you to be a deeper and more purpose-oriented leader. For most people, that kind of calling is prompted. Most of us don't start to analyze out of the blue. Usually something in our lives is a catalyst to that calling. And that catalyst prompts an urge to lead a meaningful life, opening us up to life's deeper questions of "Who am I really? Why am I here? And what is the best use of my time?" If we stay with these questions long enough, we start to form an intention. And we simultaneously notice which parts of our old reality our ego is holding on to. The truth is, our ego is not going to be letting go of control that easily, especially when there are gains or benefits to some of those old ways of being. So you start to catch it out, you learn to stay humble with it, and you start trusting yourself. Trust turns out to be a good thing, and you get new benefits that feel more meaningful than the old, ego-based ones. Then you travel up the axis of the Compass and begin to learn more.

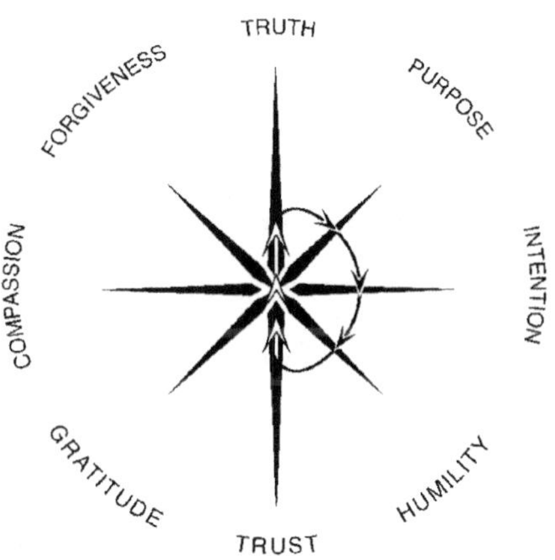

A friend of mine shared that a similar faith had guided her when she started an emergency food organization in New York in the first two weeks of the global pandemic. New York was hit exceptionally hard with food insecurity at that time, and it was reported that—as businesses folded and restaurants shut down—over one-third of the city didn't know where their next meal was coming from. Starting an organization under those conditions was challenging, but when I asked my friend what the core component was, she told me it was faith. "We didn't have any government funding because we were a new organization, so we had to rely on donations and the goodwill of others," she shared. It became a running joke in her organization that whenever someone asked how much money they had left, the answer was always "Enough for two weeks more." After one year of operation they had cooked over 100,000 hot meals with the faith that there was always going to be enough, even when it seemed that funds would run out. They are still going strong today, now standing as a fully fledged non-profit organization, and she puts one of the biggest components of their success down to the fact that they operated without any fear and with trust and faith as a guiding principle.

It's worth noting that when I talked through the Inner Compass with her, it became clear that she had implemented all of the prior aspects of the Compass before she arrived at trust. She was already someone who had been working extensively on her ego, and she had an in-depth understanding of the survival mechanism in her brain. As far as purpose goes, prior to the pandemic she had already been deeply affected by the food insecurity issues in New York, and she had set an intention to make an impact on those issues, and had been doing so on a smaller scale for a while. The pandemic accelerated her into further action. So when it came to trust, she was very easily able to get to that place because she had already done the groundwork.

THE ILLUSION OF CONTROL

There is another requirement for trust to be activated, and that is the letting go of control. Our ego likes to tell us that control is the solution to everything. Yet if we had the ability to be honest with ourselves, very little is actually in our control. Yes, we can set intentions and work towards them, but the realm in which they exist is not one we actually have control over. Every moment we spend convincing ourselves that we can control things is a waste of our time and energy. *Our true freedom comes when we let go of the illusion of control and behave intentionally, but without being attached to the outcome.* Our illusion of control comes from the ego. "I'll try to control you, and if I can't, I won't trust you." The ego divides the world into those we think we can control (and therefore trust), and those we can't control (and therefore don't trust).

We can connect this trust element to Daniel Pink's research on what creates drive. If you think back to chapter 3, we highlighted that the three elements of drive were purpose, mastery and autonomy. In other words, allowing me to do something valuable and meaningful, helping me become good at it and then trusting me to do the job within a given framework. When employees feel that trust has been taken away from them, they become demotivated. It goes something like: "When someone doesn't trust me, it says that in some ways I am less than what they expected. And that comes to: Am I worthy enough? So when you don't trust me, you are saying that I am not right, which makes me feel unworthy. Then why should I stay motivated?" In contrast, when someone does something meaningful and feels trusted, *that's* when they feel motivated.

Leaders who micromanage are the ones who don't trust others. It is actually a very selfish act to be a distrustful micromanager. Someone who is managing in this way is only looking out for themselves. They will say they are looking out for the company's interest, but they are really exercising their ego-based control issues. We could even map the journey of a micromanager as follows:

FEAR → LOOKING FOR CERTAINTY → CONTROL → MICROMANAGE

In contrast, an Inner Compass leader says, "That is not the mission we are on. I choose to see everyone as being whole. I choose to promote purpose and intention over control and minimizing others. I choose to be a role model for trust, by showing my team that I trust them. I'm going to harness the drive that comes with giving my team autonomy and purpose. I'm going to act as a coach and mentor and support my team to become masters, understanding that others feel inspired when they build their skills and improve on them."

HOW TRUST RELATES TO THE OTHER ELEMENTS OF THE COMPASS

When you move through the upcoming side of the Compass, trust is going to gain an even broader dimension. I can briefly describe that dimension to you here, but as you already know, the Inner Compass works experientially, and you will need to actually go through the other aspects of the Compass to broaden that trust. But if you are operating from an increased sense of trust, when we go back up the truth axis, you are likely going to have a greater understanding of your ego and your patterns, and encounter more limitations that you can let go of. We're also going to move into forgiveness in the next chapter, and it's going to work hand-in-hand with trust, because you will trust yourself enough to forgive, and likely find that you start to become freer than you can remember being in a long time. Additionally, we'll move into compassion, and trust will enable you to develop more compassion for yourself and others. You will start to recognize that everyone is dealing with the same 'demons' so your compassion will be increased. And the more you trust yourself to let go, the more your gratitude increases, and you start to feel this underlying joy at the immense opportunity that is your life. So you trust that if you seek more truth, you can have more of these elements, and together they begin to expand. Your trust gains the insight that comes from forgiveness, compassion and gratitude. You start to extend that same compassion to those around you. You recognize, more and more, that your team members are also people who are on a journey with baggage that they might want to let go of. With this understanding comes gratitude. If you are able to sit and feel grateful for all the insights you have gained into people and the way they are, you start to realize that you want to trust them and help to build them up. You choose to trust them and see them as already whole.

Johann Wolfgang von Goethe famously said, "If you treat an individual as he is, he will remain how he is. But if you treat him as if he were what he ought to be and could be, he will become what he ought to be and could be." This is Inner Compass because when you distrust, you keep people weak. But the other path offers them an opportunity to step up and become what they can be.

Now that we've identified trust as a core component of your Inner Compass journey, in the next chapter we'll move into forgiveness, so you can figure out

what you need to let go of, so you can trust even more.

CHAPTER 7
FORGIVENESS

Forgiveness is giving up the hope that the past could have been any different, it's accepting the past for what it was, and using this moment and this time to help yourself move forward. **Oprah Winfrey**

Forgiveness is the fuel for letting go. Many people say they have nothing to forgive, and although in some cases that might be true, most of us have baggage that we've been carrying for so long, we don't even know it's there.

Forgiveness has two core components: Forgiving ourselves and forgiving others. When we don't forgive ourselves, we project guilt and shame inwardly. And when we don't forgive others, we project resentment and blame outwardly. These are destructive forces that take up a tremendous amount of energy and resources.

When we learn to forgive, it creates a freedom that allows the emergence of our soul. The outer ego layers that have been covering it are lifted away. Your burden becomes lighter when all of a sudden your inner self no longer carries all this extra weight.

For the Inner Compass, humility and forgiveness are on the same axis for a reason. Humility and forgiveness are the elements that give us a kind of unspoken depth to our character. When we are able to be humble and forgive, we move out of our ego-led characteristics of being right and defending our point of view. We acknowledge the challenges that everyone faces in navigating being human, and we find the courage to see beyond our triggers and our self-righteousness. We also need humility to enter into forgiveness. This includes being humble with what you know and also what you don't know. It also includes being humble when faced with the feeling of being wronged. This chapter will bring together many of the previous elements of the Compass with a slightly different focus. So far, much of the Inner Compass work has been self-exploratory, but with this element, we focus much more on how this element impacts our experience with others.

The Inner Compass leader who has learned to forgive and let go can operate more dynamically in stressful times. They experience less pressure. They keep a calmer head and are more present in each meeting. *They learn to let go and forgive and this takes away the very proof that the ego needs in order to justify its existence.* That is the key to forgiveness on this journey and its role in the Inner Compass.

MOVING INTO FORGIVENESS WITH YOUR INNER COMPASS JOURNEY

At this point on your Inner Compass path, you've looked within and explored how your truth has been shaped by your experiences. You've clarified why you are here and set the intention for purposeful living. You've worked on becoming more humble and developing humility. You've gone deep within so you can experience a greater sense of trust. And although we've been doing some work on how you relate to your team members, the forgiveness work takes it up a notch in terms of your interactions with others in your world. Here we shoot up the axis of the Inner Compass. As we do, we go deeper into ourselves, and we lighten the burden, letting go and forgiving.

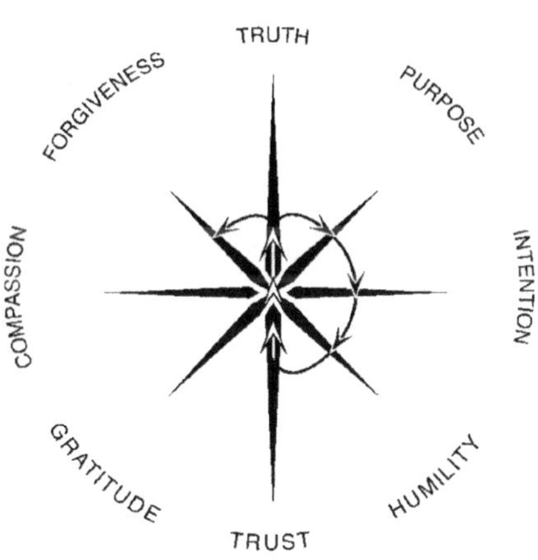

You could say that this aspect (and the two that follow) are the more "spiritual" elements of the Compass. Again, I'm not referring to organized religion, but more the idea of connecting with something that is greater than ourselves. When I teach this part in my seminars, I tell the participants that they will roughly divide into two groups: the ones who see this as spiritual and the ones who just see this as a deeper and different psychological dive into who they are. And I make the point that it does not much matter which it is, as long as it helps us grow and mature as human beings and as leaders. The same applies to you. Whether you consider yourself to be someone who is exploring more of the spiritual aspects or the psychological aspects of yourself, these elements will give you the depth to grow as a leader.

There is a lot of talk in both spiritual and psychological circles about forgiveness, because it's widely understood that if you release the burdens of your past, you make way for a different kind of living. The quality of your life changes as you are holding on to less pain than you were before. The truth is though, that *there can also be a tendency to speak of forgiveness without actually living it, and to counter this, we have to ensure that truth and forgiveness work together simultaneously.* Someone might go to their therapist and be told that there is great freedom when they forgive. They might pay lip service to forgiving the mistakes of the past, or force a sense of forgiveness, but not actually *feel* that forgiveness inside of them. And this is where we have to get really precise with our truth and become highly aware, because forgiveness definitely can't be a concept or a box that we've ticked. If we simultaneously say we have forgiven ourselves or others while secretly harboring resentment, we actually find ourselves moving further from our truth. We create a division in ourselves between what is real and what we would like to be real. So, *forgiveness cannot be an act of the ego. It has to be an act of the soul.* And we have to be working with a heightened level of self-awareness to be able to tell the difference.

WHAT ARE WE ACTUALLY FORGIVING?

It can be helpful to understand that what we are often forgiving—in ourselves and others—are unconscious acts carried out by the protective layers of the ego. *Ego keeps pointing to the incidents that hurt us for the justification of its existence.* When we can begin to see that this is how the ego behaves, we understand—with compassion—that it clings like a child to parts of us that no longer serve our greater selves.

Perhaps one of the greatest models of moving to forgiveness can be seen in the teachings of Nelson Mandela. He said, "Resentment is like drinking poison and then hoping it will kill your enemies." When we resent those who we perceive have wronged us, what we are actually doing is resenting their ego patterns and creating suffering for ourselves because of these patterns.

There are several methods—mental, spiritual and emotional—of getting to forgiveness. The following four approaches look at this from all these different angles and you'll probably find that one approach resonates with you more than another. Whichever approach you take, it's essential that you get to the feeling of forgiveness: of moving beyond just the concept of it.

METHODS FOR GETTING TO FORGIVENESS

Method One: Mantra. Create a mantra that you use in meditation.

You will literally create a line of text about forgiving yourself for a specific act, or forgiving someone you feel has wronged you. You repeat this line over and over again (60 times in one sitting) for as long as it takes for it to be true. This may feel odd, but it has worked for countless people. The sitting takes place daily, and most people feel the letting go happen around the 30-day mark. You'll know that it has happened when the statement goes from a mechanical saying that you repeat, to something that you actually feel to be true.

Method Two: Prayer. "I pray that this resentment be taken away from me." This one is a heartfelt prayer that you repeat until, again, the feeling of resentment is gone.

Method Three: Evoking Emotions. This is partner work where you evoke emotions through active support from your partner. A lot of the time your resentment is there as an underlying feeling that you haven't either fully recognized or processed. Working with a partner encourages you to let the feeling rise and be as big as it wants to be, so that you can process it and move on. Let's say it's anger, and your partner encourages you to allow it to become as big as it wants to be. As you feel and let out the anger, a release of emotional energy happens. Then the anger subsides. Next, your partner asks "What's there now?" Perhaps there will be something like despair. Again, your partner encourages you to let the despair become as big as it wants to: even if it overpowers you. Then allow despair to become as big as it needs to be. Then fear (which is usually the driving force of anger) may come to the forefront and you allow that to become as big as it needs to be. This is a bit of an exhaustive process, but what usually happens is you get to a state of being that feels more benevolent. Possibly calmness, then peace. Finally your partner asks you, "What's there?" And you get to joy. So what usually happens is that you keep working through these layers until you are finally in a blissful state, where you feel completely at ease, happy, content, and as though you are floating. But again, this can't be forced and it definitely takes time and dedicated work.

Method Four: The Calm Lake of Forgiveness.

(This exercise is also partner work.)

I recommend you have a guide with you in your discussion with whoever you would like to forgive. Also, invite the younger version of yourself, at the age when the incident happened.

You leave the shore of a calm lake in a rowboat. Gliding on the still lake in beautiful weather, you feel enveloped by the spirit of loving kindness.

The person or group you want to forgive leaves in their boat from the opposite shore and you meet in the middle with a comfortable distance between you. Your partner reminds you that you are enveloped by the lake's spirit of loving kindness and that you have come here to explore forgiveness. This is not to say that what happened was OK, but with the possibility of forgiving the other person's soul and allowing yourself to let go of the grievance, for your own sake.

When you are ready, your partner asks you to sincerely explain (out loud) to the person(s) in the other boat how you experienced what happened, how it hurt you and how you feel about it. The younger version of yourself also gets to have their say in this.

Then the other party gets to say their side of the story and your partner asks you to say the words that the other person says. You speak them out loud. Your guide asks you to allow this person to speak from the heart, so that you can see the younger version of yourself and the entire incident through their eyes.

As the conversation develops further, your guide reminds you of the spirit of loving kindness and encourages you to say all that needs to be said, recommending you allow the other person to do the same.

Finally, your partner asks you if you are ready to forgive the other person and if you are, you speak your words out loud.

This exercise can have a massive effect on people's lives, and deeply transform the way that they relate to those who hurt them.

When you go through this work, be it through mantra, prayer or emotions—particularly when you release the feelings you were holding on to—you allow the emergence of your true self and your core. It's like you have this rock, covered with all this mud; its surface has been hidden for years, and suddenly you decide to clean it off and your cleaning reveals a beauty you had no idea existed.

Some of your relationships and memories will need a deeper process than others. But the more you can let go of, the more you start to see this core, the more you can act from your true inner self, without the protective ego layers ruling the show. In that sense, forgiveness is freedom because it allows the emergence of your true self and your core. I had this experience working through my relationship with my mother. My mother is an incredible human being who, as a young woman, was an accomplished ballerina. She was raised to "do things right" by her parents. In addition, she was—to a great extent—raised by strong German women who lived with the family as housemaids. These women were World War II survivors who encouraged my mother to be strong, and insisted that she should raise her own children with this strength too. My mother passed this strength on to me. She cared for me greatly, but we weren't a family that expressed much affection. As a result, when it came to my own relationships, I found myself looking for women who either did not need much affection, or at least accepted receiving little affection from me. Until I did the forgiveness process on my mother, I didn't realize I needed something else—my whole world around relationships shifted when I did this work. And the irony was, after doing the forgiveness work, I understood that my mother had only brought me up in that way

because she wanted me to be strong and wanted the best for me. So the forgiveness process can enable us to see the bigger picture of those in our lives and understand them better.

Underneath it all, whenever you let go of these resentments—all this blame, all this guilt and shame—you are letting go of a lot of the patterns that justified your being driven by fear. When they are gone, you really see how holding on to those grudges and not wanting to forgive was counterproductive to you. And when you are no longer governed by those patterns, there is no justification to listen to that fear-based voice, and it eventually fades away.

Gaining access to your inner self changes everything in leadership. Earlier I highlighted that humility and forgiveness are on the same axis, and they are the yin that makes the yang work. *Humility manages the ego. Then with forgiveness, we completely disarm the ego by letting go of the pain that was holding it in place.*

YOU CAN FORGIVE THE PERSON WITHOUT CONDONING THE ACT

Many years ago in Iceland, I had a business partner and we didn't part ways very well. He bought me out in a way that wasn't fair and I held on to a grudge for years. With conscious effort and significant work, I forgave his core for what his ego did. I didn't forgive the act itself, but I understood what journey that human being was on and through humility I learned to see that journey in the light of forgiveness and compassion.

In the same vein, a lot of people who come to my seminars have experienced violence on some level. When they know the forgiveness component is coming on the seminar they often say, "I'm not sure I want to forgive." Again, I remind them that they are not forgiving the act of violence itself. They are forgiving the ego patterns of the one who committed it, with the compassion and understanding of where those patterns came from. And again, this work can't be forced.

If I believe everyone has a core that is benevolent and loving, then that core suffers the follies and errors of the ego because of the way we are raised and function as a society and as a species. We listen very strongly to the ego and we need maturity to listen to our core. We are all on a journey where we make endless mistakes, and the fact that one of yours may have impacted me is just life. I forgive you. And I move on.

FORGIVING YOUR EMPLOYEES, COLLEAGUES, AND DIFFICULT BOSSES

When you are this far in the Compass and you have begun to gain freedom from your own patterns and fear, you start to notice these ego-based patterns in your team members too. Let's say you have a team member who constantly compares—someone on your team that either overtly or covertly says, "Is my status comparable to other people who work here?" You start to see patterns. If their status is OK, it means they are safe. If they haven't reached a higher status in a fixed time frame they think they will be unsuccessful, which means they feel unsafe. So they'll do whatever is needed to protect or enhance their status.

You'll also recognize these patterns in colleagues who are on the same level as you, who possibly sought to trip you up in an attempt to surpass you in the race towards the top. These kinds of patterns are inevitable when individuals are operating from survival and want to create safety for themselves. This extends to difficult bosses as well. This is an especially relevant topic in ego-driven organizations where front line and middle managers can feel helpless towards dominant—and often aggressive—senior managers.

You'll also start to recognize these patterns in your team members. But equally, you'll begin to be a role model by not engaging in these behaviors yourself. You'll start to compassionately call out these behaviors, and set expectations for a different culture, because ultimately, you will want to establish a culture that is free of these ego behaviors—and that has to start with you.

In contrast, ego-driven leaders will always exploit these fears, because that's what gives them additional drive. They will subconsciously say, "I hate being afraid. I'll do whatever I can to not feel afraid," yet they will simultaneously use all kinds of fear tactics with those they employ. *Ego wants to feel powerful and it will never admit that fear is its driver.* And if it has to admit it, it will say it outsmarts fear.

You'll see ego-driven managers who feel it is important to have the big car, the promotion, the house by the lake—but none of those status symbols hold for long when their fear is unresolved. Instead, there is an empty feeling. There is also an imposter syndrome that the ego just can't get past. "I don't have it together. I'm going to get found out," their inner voice will say. "What if my coping strategies don't hold?" Whereas if you reach the core and you are in that state where you have released the trappings of the ego—largely through trust, forgiveness and letting go—you are able to rest in that space where there is no fear. Instead, your mindset will be "Whatever my flaws are, I am human, I have let go of the things that I need to let go of, I am standing in my truth." And you stand as the person that you are today with the knowledge that you have done all you can to address the trappings of the past. You tip from being fear-driven to being purpose-driven and open to possibility.

In a business context, if you are an Inner Compass leader and you have gotten to this point, you don't hold grudges either. You can go into a project with someone who let you down previously and expect them to be a new person in that scenario. That's what people sense from a leader who can let go and forgive. When people make mistakes, with you they will get a true second chance (as opposed to when the second chance is granted but the leader secretly harbors a lack of trust in them). And not only that, but when an Inner Compass leader has done the process of forgiving and letting go, and they are in touch with their core, it's almost as if the people around them can see their core. And when they see this or sense this, they want some of it. Think about what effect that has when a manager gives everyone a second chance to be themselves and get it right. When people feel free it inspires them. "I am getting a second chance. He/she/they must see some worth in me." And ultimately your teams will function so much more effectively because they won't be on edge all the time.

Now that we've seen the power of forgiveness on both a personal and interpersonal level, and how this can affect the function of your teams, we've begun to clear the way for the next two chapters, which move us into what might be considered the more gracious aspects of humanity. We'll look at exploring the two core components of compassion and gratitude, which are aspirational qualities that tend to bring us more joy and happiness, and we'll begin to sincerely evolve the way you show up as a leader with these qualities at your core.

FOUTH SEGMENT

EMBRACING MY INNER SELF

PART 5

CHAPTER 8
COMPASSION

Love and compassion are necessities, not luxuries. Without them, humanity cannot survive. **Dalai Lama**

At the start of the global pandemic, Annabel was a finance manager working for a high-end auction site based in New York City. In the first week of the COVID-19 lockdown, Annabel felt disappointed by her company's ethics when they'd tried to use the backdrop of the pandemic to manipulate more sales. Their "Stuck at home? At least surround yourself with shiny objects," campaign had seemed shallow, crass and tone-deaf to Annabel, especially as New York was so hard hit in those first few weeks when COVID reached the city. What followed, though, was a display of leadership that was ten times more shocking to her, and a moment she will never forget. One morning, two weeks into lockdown, a team meeting was announced on Zoom. "We're making cutbacks due to COVID," the CEO told them abruptly on the call, and without any warning. "By the time I hang up, half of you will be gone." In an unbelievably callus display of management, as the call ended, names started disappearing from the Slack channel in a quick-fire elimination round. Employees frantically messaged each other, trying to figure out which of them were staying and who had lost their jobs. Already dealing with survival issues due to the intensity of the pandemic, members of the team were thrust into a deeper level of survival by losing their income sources in such a cold and heartless manner. Although Annabel was one of the employees who still had a job at the end of that day, she started a job search a few weeks later, as did the majority of her remaining colleagues. She changed companies as soon as she could with a vow that she would never stay in an environment that so significantly lacked compassion.

It is likely no surprise to you that at this stage of your Inner Compass work, a lack of compassion can be traced back to ego. The ego builds its whole world on separateness, and in the world of ego, there is a "me" who I must take care of and "the others" who aren't my concern. If I'm wrapped up in my ego, if the whole world revolves around me and my safety, then why should I care how others feel and whether their needs are met? This is how ego builds its world, and there isn't any room for compassion when it does. Compassion is a quality that is also included in ego-based misconceptions. Someone who is operating from ego will likely tell you that compassion costs too much energy and there is no gain.

Yet compassion is one of our highest human qualities. According to extensive neuroscience studies carried out by Buddhist teacher Roshi Joan Halifax, compassion lights up the whole brain on a fundamental level. Halifax's body of work shows that operating from compassion is not only trainable from a neuroscience perspective—it also does not require self-sacrifice. Instead it increases our well-being, along with the well-being of those that we support.

In this chapter, we're going to take a look at how to operate from this higher human quality. For the Inner Compass, compassion is on the same axis as intention for a reason: it needs to be a driving force. With a combination of the teachings that have gone before, we have been carving a path to compassion, and in this part of the journey we look at how we can evolve into being a more compassionate leader and being.

DEFINING COMPASSION

We can define compassion as recognizing the suffering of others. It's not that you suffer with them—it's more that you have the capacity to feel what they are feeling in their own suffering. It's non-judgmentally being there for them. Some people confuse compassion with pity but the two have different qualities. Pity is still a form of judgment. It's the ego perceiving someone else to have less than. Compassion has a completely different quality. It's the quality of "I feel what you feel. I feel with you and I am here." Sometimes it means actively helping in that situation, and other times just fully being there and showing that you feel what another person feels is help in itself.

INNER COMPASS: HOW THE JOURNEY SO FAR LEADS US TO COMPASSION

Many people try to be outwardly compassionate without developing self-compassion, but—like all the other aspects of the Inner Compass journey—we have to begin with self-compassion before we can operate authentically with others.

At this stage on your Inner Compass path, we have taken steps to develop your humility and to ensure that you are working towards being more humble. If you have managed to be the observer of your own ego patterns, you have by now started to become more and more aware of when the ego takes over, and also when it releases its grip. In an iconic interview with Oprah Winfrey, Eckhart Tolle talks about how the ego first shows its face.[1] Tolle explains that, "It first starts with the toy when the baby reaches for it, and the toy is taken away and the child says, *'That's Mine.'*" Tolle calls this "The beginning of identification with things." Oprah replied that as we get older the toys just get bigger. I have a Jeep. A wife. Kids. A house. These are all bigger than Lego, but

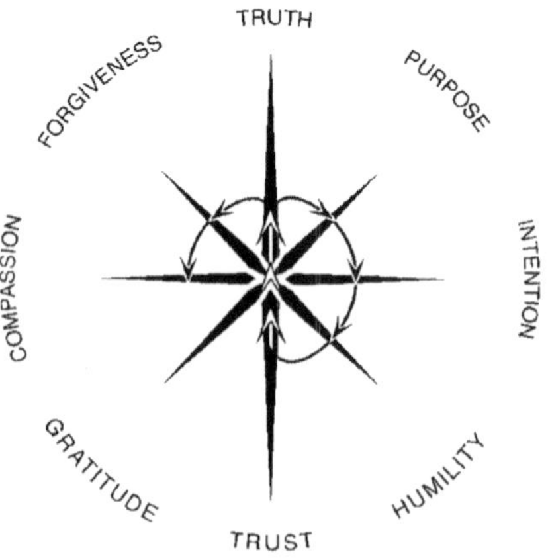

the principle is the same. Tolle goes on to highlight that as soon as there is an attachment, we fall into the trap of me against the world and a separateness is created. He explains, "Ego is always just identification with one form or another. A physical form. My house, my car and so on. So that when you identify, the sense of who you are is in that thing. And if that thing is criticized, you become defensive or threatened because you feel your very sense of self is threatened. But then there are other forms of identification, for example, my opinions and mental positions . . . I am right. And that implies that somebody else has to be wrong." And this is essentially where the formation of our ego begins.

Ego is also about the identification with the story of who you tell yourself you are. It's a culmination of everything that has happened in your life including your successes and failures, your tragedies and victories. It's the way that you have identified with all that and how it defines you. As you start to break down the ego you simultaneously discover, "This is why I am the way I am," and "If it's all just a story, then I can free myself from this story." You begin to get glimpses that the story is not the real you. You start to connect with your inner core. From your truth, you set a clear purpose and intention, and then likely you see how ego has a tendency to derail your plans. As you start to get a grip on your patterns, then you also begin to trust that things will go OK.

Once we learn to let go of the things that have happened to us, we remove the foundation that ego is built upon, and let go of story altogether. All the stories of being wronged and treated unfairly, all the injustices and the blame: once you embrace humility and trust in the face of these past events and learn to let them go, then you open up to your full capacity for compassion. So you have done the groundwork which enables a major heart opening of this journey. Once you've recognized your own suffering, you can reach a place where you speak to yourself without judgment and are deeply present with yourself. This is what is truly meant by self-love, and compassion towards others is usually limited until you've embraced that compassion within yourself.

For most of us, especially those who have been used to being high achievers, that self-compassion does not come easily. When I was getting divorced, I was working on an important project for Microsoft. I was also seeing a psychologist to support me through the divorce. When I complained to her that my project wasn't going well, she said, "Wait, you are in the middle of a divorce. Are you saying that you didn't expect your work to suffer?" The truth of it was that I hadn't. I was so armored that I wasn't allowing any compassion for myself. Back then, my common approach was to press on regardless, and it left little room for a self-compassionate stance.

Like most of these patterns, a similar theme was present from childhood. I was born with a clubbed foot, but I got it fixed early on. My mom trained me hard so that I could experience a 'normal life' and I went into sports, pushing my way into anything that I could do. Years later in my late 40s, I found myself in a yoga class, and as

I stretched, I connected deeply to the problems that I'd experienced all my life with my legs. I'd had multiple surgeries. I'd been twisted and torn. And I realized that the little child in me was still angry and disappointed with my legs and that I'd treated them badly all my life. I'd not given them any care or shown them any love. I just expected them to perform. In some ways, I'd treated them like a dissociated part of myself. In that class I found myself speaking to my legs and admitting that I had not treated them well. In recognizing and integrating that part of myself, it evoked a feeling of self-compassion that my body had suffered. When you show up with presence of mind and fully acknowledge a part of you that you may have been unconsciously rejecting, it can have a profound healing effect. You know when you've made a mistake. You know that your younger self developed coping strategies that didn't necessarily serve you as an adult. You have compassion for that part of yourself that didn't know any better. And the part of you that felt separate or wrong gets integrated. This is when you start to feel whole, because you are collecting all these parts of yourself that you felt were wrong and you are bringing them into a place of love and acceptance. Then, and only then, can you start to project authentic compassion out to others. And because you have lived it for yourself, others will sense that it is real.

WHY COMPASSION IS ESSENTIAL FOR LEADERSHIP

After a devastating terror attack in Christchurch, New Zealand, where 50 Muslims were shot as they prayed, the extraordinarily compassionate response of their Prime Minister, Jacinda Ardern, brought her to the center of the world stage.

She told the terrorists, “You may have chosen us, but we utterly reject and condemn you.” While meeting Muslim leaders, she wore a black headscarf to note her respect. She also refused to focus on Islamophobia as the root cause of the attack, and instead, she was willing to look at the deeper, underlying causes of what occurred. The whole world watched as she responded with compassion. Simultaneously, many of us paused to reflect on how it would be if we had consistent compassionate global leadership of this kind.

Previously the yin and yang of business was highlighted. Compassion is aimed at alleviating suffering and can be ferocious as well as tender, yang as well as yin. It’s the mother gently comforting her crying child or the mother bear fiercely protecting her cubs. You can see this in a leader such as Ardern in the way that she combines humility with strength. She is humble enough to be someone who is known to put her family at the forefront and still lead a country. She is trusting enough to make tough decisions. And she is deeply guided by a sense of compassion that is almost palpable when you see her in action. When we see a leader such as Ardern in action, it’s not surprising that when Gallup asked people around the world what they look for in a leader, compassion came up in the top four.

While what Ardern models can be seen in her running of a country, she also models the kind of compassion needed to lead an organization.

Compassion in leadership is about having an awareness of what your people are going through. But it is also so much more. It's about how you handle the mistakes of your employees too. Your people want to feel respected, acknowledged and supported. But they also don't want to feel rejected when they make a mistake (which at some point, they will inevitably do). The grace with which you treat your employees when they make a mistake is a vital component to how you lead.

When we are scolded for making mistakes in life, it triggers us into survival mode. Some people have a really strong survival mechanism which dominates their home life so completely that every time they argue with their partner, they visualize the relationship ending and them being left with no one. Others have a strong survival mechanism which predominates in the workplace. A mistake at work can spiral them into visions of losing their job and ultimately being out on the streets. These spiraling catastrophic visions of failure and rejection can be deeply entrenched, and some people have a greater sensitivity to them than others, depending on how severely their survival mechanisms were activated in childhood. As a leader, the more compassion you can have for your team members, the more you understand them as humans and acknowledge their human condition, the safer they will feel, and the more time they can actually spend on getting their work done. Treating them with compassion invokes a sense of safety, which means that your team will function much more efficiently than if you are constantly triggering them.

The embracing of humility and forgiveness that you have been working on so far has given you a bit of space between the inner you and the patterns that you were used to operating from. And in that space, you start to see the patterns in those around you. When one of your team is stuck in their ego patterns—the perfectionist, the winner, the people-pleaser, the joker—you feel compassion for where they are. This includes understanding, respect, and having the ability to feel how they feel.

Acting with compassion doesn't mean that you can't call out these challenging behaviors. But the way you do that will likely transform. If you have someone on your team ruffling everyone's feathers, you recognize their ego is out of control but that's where they need to be on their journey. You show compassion for them. You still call out the behavior but you do it in a way that understands their behavior (without condoning it). You find a way to connect with the why behind their actions, rather than simply condemning what they said.

COMPASSION IN COMPANIES

Compassion becomes critical when you are working in a company that is going through significant change. The uncertainty, confusion and the volatility of the global pandemic have highlighted the need for more compassionate leaders in business, particularly as jobs have been cut and uncertainty has reigned. We opened this chapter with a story about a CEO who cut half his workforce during one Zoom meeting at the height of the COVID-19 pandemic, and we can now look at what might be occurring in a scenario of this nature from another angle. If we identify too strongly with our ego and we have no connection to our inner core, we become deeply embedded in our story. If that story is based on fear and separateness, it comes with a sense that "I'm alone and I need to fight for what's mine." And from that place, we have no access to compassion when we need it. We have armored ourselves so strongly that when we find ourselves in those situations we can deliver the news that, "By the end of this meeting half of you will be gone," without any attempt to soften the blow, because our outer layers are so thick that we don't have access to our compassion or the impact of our words. Brené Brown calls this approach "armored leadership." In *Dare to Lead* she shares "to be the person who we long to be—we must again be vulnerable. We must take off the armor, put down the weapons, show up, and let ourselves be seen." An uncompassionate leader is so caught up in the protection of their armor that they don't even know how to consider leading beyond it.

Now contrast the above story to one of a CTO I worked with who was going through a difficult change in digitalization. She shared with her team: "We've made a difficult decision. We are securing everyone's jobs but the servicing of our systems will be outsourced." She explained this to them with tears in her eyes. Those who were present had expected strong reactions including people walking out the door, and protesting about being moved. But because of her authenticity and the fact that she showed compassion, her people responded gracefully.

My own company grew exponentially in the pandemic. It was partly because, as I mentioned earlier, I hired an awesome manager whose

approach was exactly what the team needed in those challenging times. She gave my team so much support and there was a sense that everyone on my team was giving it their best. I didn't need to micromanage and we got more things right than wrong. There was hardly any space for the team to breathe and she showed great understanding of the survival fears that the pandemic brought. A guiding force was the compassion we had for our team and the respect that we had that they would show up and do the best they could. This manager is still with us and continues to lead the team with compassion. And her influence and impact is growing by every quarter that goes by.

Now that we have explored compassion as a vital element of the Inner Compass, you are likely getting the sense that at this stage, there is a first heart opening towards love. Humility gives us the ability to approach everyone respectfully, to listen, to grow with them, and to connect to that feeling of oneness. When we connect to that sense of oneness, we see that being part of a team is so much more than fulfilling tasks. It's about connecting on a deeper human level so that we can understand one another and grow together. The Inner Compass is really about moving from separateness and fear to love and compassion. And the next and final element of the Compass is gratitude, and how we can live and lead with our hearts on fire with appreciation in every single moment.

CHAPTER 9
GRATITUDE

It is through gratitude for the present moment that the spiritual dimension of life opens up. **Eckhart Tolle**

When I was 22, I had a near-death experience. I was 10 days from going to a university in the US, and before I left, I went celebrating with a few friends. Somewhere in our drunken celebrations we decided to drive from Reykjavik to a country festival in the middle of the night. Halldor, my friend, had a state-of-the-art Range Rover, and since I wasn't as drunk as he was, I took the wheel. As we drove to the destination, we crossed a couple of creeks. We felt the power of the Range Rover beneath us in the water, and something inside us clicked. We decided to test how well the Range Rover could cross a larger river. When I pass that same river today I realize how drunk we must have been because the river in question was huge.

Halldor was in the passenger seat, and as I coursed the car towards the riverbank, he realized it was too steep. He jumped from the car, and I hit the brakes as hard as I could. I felt responsible in the driver's seat, and at that moment, my instinct to save the car was stronger than my understanding of the danger I was in. I thought that the car would quickly hit the ground and stop. It wasn′t until the car was in the middle of the river, floating like a boat with the water up to my waist, that I realized the severity of the situation. At that moment I called out to my father with gut-wrenching fear.

As the car floated along down the river, the electric windows no longer worked, so I couldn't get out. The car rolled over, the roof was crushed down into the seats with me still inside, and then it righted itself. I remember punching the windows and screaming. I remember not wanting to die. The strange thing was, I have no recollection of how I got onto the roof. But I did have all the hallmarks of a near-death experience before I got there, including seeing a tunnel of light.

Eventually I was rescued by a family that had been camping nearby. Because I was intoxicated, I wasn't taken to the hospital. Instead, I got put straight into jail. All the money I had saved for the university went towards paying for the car. I was fortunate enough to have grandparents who lent me the initial money needed for my studies, otherwise I wouldn't have been able to go.

Ten days later I was alone in the States. No post-traumatic therapy.

No help. Not surprisingly, the two components I picked to study were psychology and religion. I couldn't figure out why I didn't die and everyone who saw what had happened said it was incomprehensible that I had survived.

The downside of the experience is that I felt very driven. It gave me an overwhelming sense that I was here for a reason, and I struggled for some time to rectify that feeling with my choices, and the debt I felt I owed to life. The upside, though, was an overwhelming sense of gratitude that started almost immediately. I'd sit in the library of the university watching squirrels running up trees, and I would cry with gratitude. I had a newfound feeling of excitement for this life, how amazing it can be, and the impact I can make. I still feel that sense of excitement prominently today.

THE ENERGY OF GRATITUDE

So, here's what I am *not* talking about when I say gratitude: John calls and says "Thanks for the great job you did yesterday. Have a great weekend." That's appreciation, but it's not the depth of gratitude I am referring to. I'm talking about that heartfelt, lip-quivering, deep-seated feeling of "I can't believe how grateful I am," that permeates every cell.

What is the energy that comes with gratitude? You could say that it's a kind of inner warmth: studies have shown that gratitude practices help connection with others and strengthen relationships, well-being and happiness. There's also an open-heartedness that comes with it. A sense of being part of something greater and a willingness to openly express that feeling. It's generative. It's forward-moving and expansive. It's a sincere, "Thank you that I can be part of this. How can I contribute?" It casts off the protection of the ego which is focused on "me and mine," and opens up the energy of the heart to "us and ours."

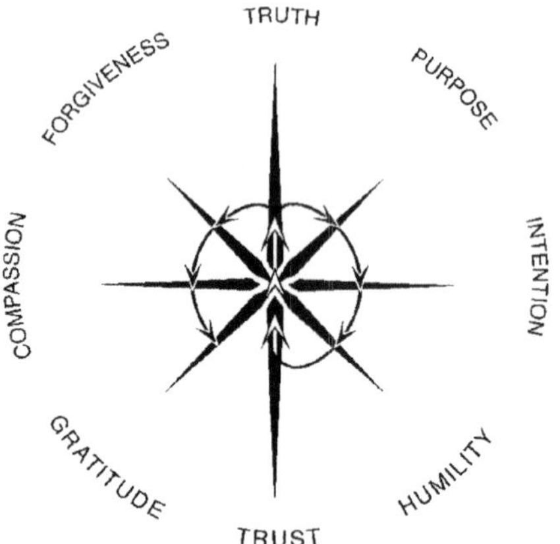

Gratitude makes you want to engage with life more. On the surface, it can seem like we are just talking about positive thinking. We have all likely had the experience in life where we choose to see and focus on the positives, and the feeling of positivity grows inside us. We've also likely all experienced the reverse, where we are looking at life through the lens of negativity and that starts to grow. With gratitude, it's not just about positive thinking. It's about positive feeling. Again, not a feeling that is forced or feigned, but one that we are generating through our commitment to ourselves to being utterly grateful for being on this planet, in this moment in time, with these experiences— to be willing to engage with those experiences with curiosity and an open heart, to see what's possible from that stance. Some people naturally feel this quality. Others have to work on it. But results can be surprisingly effective if we are consistent. Millions of people around the world have done something as simple as writing down three things that they are grateful for each day, and many have marveled at how this simple act can make such a profound difference in perception and feeling, rewiring their perception to experience and feel reality on a completely different level.

At the start of working with gratitude, we might get specific moments that are punctuated by it. Sometimes there are moments of gratitude that knock you off your feet. For example, I was sitting at the dinner table with my wife and our combined six children. There were a couple of our kids' boyfriends at the table too. I couldn't believe how grateful I was that these amazing young people were sitting around me. The feeling was one of overwhelming love and awe. So there might be times where it comes in waves and then leaves us again. What we are working towards, though, is making gratitude a fundamental part of the way that we show up in the world. So initially you might have more gratitude for specific people or moments in life. But that can grow to a generalized sense of gratitude for all the opportunities that we have—the challenging ones and the victorious ones. And eventually that feeling can be part of a presence that permeates your life.

HOW GRATITUDE AMPLIFIES THE OTHER ELEMENTS OF THE COMPASS

In the previous chapters on forgiveness and compassion, we looked at disarming the ego by taking away its reason for being. By forgiving ourselves and others and being both inwardly and outwardly compassionate, we move into a place where we can embrace the power of love more freely. Simultaneously, the more we focus on everything we can be grateful for, the smaller the ego gets, because there is even less for it to justify or defend.

Gratitude also further activates some of the earlier elements of the Compass, and transforms the way that those elements relate to the ego. If you take any element of the Compass, you can see how gratitude brings it to life even more. Take trust, for example. When I am grateful, I trust life more. I see all the good things that I am grateful for. I see all the growth I've had from my challenging experiences and how they've made me who I am today. It makes me trust my journey through life even more. So that soon, when I go back around the Compass again, my heart is going to be more open. "Let's find more truth. Let's keep engaging with life and seeing what else is there. So far I have discovered so many things to be grateful for. How much deeper can I go?" This approach makes you less fearful and more trusting of life, and then your heart cracks open even more.

Gratitude additionally unites with purpose in a leadership context. It sits on the same axis as gratitude, and when you find purpose for your life, you become very grateful for having a purpose. And then, when you start to work purposefully giving your best—whatever you are doing—good things start to happen. You realize you are not only grateful for having found a purpose: you become grateful for what that purpose-driven life creates. Gratitude then continually reinforces purpose and vice versa.

GRATITUDE IN A LEADERSHIP CONTEXT

When it comes to a leadership context, gratitude plays a number of vital roles. As you work with gratitude on a personal level, it starts to impact your professional life. You start to show up as a grateful leader. You are grateful that you trust yourself and have found purpose, and equally grateful for the people around you who have chosen to walk this path with you. As you develop this work further, you notice that you are becoming a more balanced, less ego-driven leader who has a calming effect on the people around you. And while these people are calm because you are not constantly triggering them into their fears and patterns, they also feel seen and valued by you, and worthy of your attention. They are not just numbers or a means to an end. They are valued human beings and part of a team you have spent time fostering and caring about. On average, people will want to stay in that kind of environment because it gives them room to grow. So essentially you are driving up job satisfaction, engagement, performance improvement and loyalty by the way you show up and interact with the people that you lead. As we've highlighted continuously with the Inner Compass work, this can't be a to-do list. There is no box checking. As a matter of fact, there is only one box that you need to check, and that is "I've discovered gratitude, and what it really means, and I've committed to living and leading from that place." (And if you are not there yet, we have some exercises at the end of this chapter to help you develop gratitude further.)

I have an example from my own team of how I acted out of gratitude for them during the height of the COVID crisis. My team did an amazing job so that not only did we survive COVID, but we thrived—strong and profitable. I looked at that team and was struck with an overwhelming sense of awe and gratitude. “What have I done to attract these people?” I thought. This group stuck with this enormous task and ensured that we grew in the most challenging of circumstances. In turn, it made me want to treat them even better. On a personal level, I continuously communicated my immense gratitude to them, and told them on a regular basis how much I cherished their efforts. I also rewarded them financially with a bonus for their efforts. Moving forward, we are redesigning our bonus scheme to reward team efforts much more than individual performance, to further emphasize that we are all in this together.

When a leader is grateful for the people they have on the team, it creates a snowball effect. You see them in a positive light, the way they show up changes, then you have more appreciation for them. People can feel it. They connect to it and contribute to it. They feel lucky. You feel lucky too. And so it grows exponentially.

HOW LIVING WITH GRATITUDE IMPACTS YOUR FAMILY

Perhaps one of my favorite examples of how living with this sense of gratitude can play out in family lives can be seen in one of my clients—the head of IT at an insurance agency—who attended a program I delivered. I'm sharing the email he sent me below (with his permission), because it exemplifies the qualities of gratitude in action.

> *Hi Thor, I'd like to share something with you. My wife was fighting cancer when I went through the leadership development program. She had reached a state of healing and then the cancer came up in her head again in Jan, 2020. Shortly after that I graduated from the leadership program. It was difficult to deliver my graduation speech. Just before my speech I had to apply first aid to my wife, and had received the news that she was terminally ill. I said to myself that if I could deliver that speech I would never have any problem standing on stage again.*
>
> *We worked together in a focused way through all of the steps of the illness. We got support from psychiatrists and peers. We discussed openly what was happening and had regular family meetings with our children.*
>
> *When my wife died, it was a beautiful moment at the hospice. My three daughters and I were allowed to stay overnight, and we were there when she drew her last breath. It was both a fond and sad memory that we will build on for life.*
>
> *I came back to work three weeks after her passing. On my second week*

back, I accepted a meeting invitation with some visiting business people, and when I got home I was exhausted—in the months leading up to my wife's death, I had used up all my resources. My fuse was short. After cooking dinner for our daughters, I saw my six- and nine-year-old kids hadn't put their clothes in their closet. I lost it and scolded them. And at that moment my oldest, who is 12, said quietly and calmly, and with lots of confidence, "Dad, this is your shadow side speaking. This pile of clothes gives you no reasons to be upset." I looked at her, smiled and told her she was absolutely right.

I explained to my daughters why I was tired and I told them what I would do to prevent coming home so tired in the future. We have regular family meetings to discuss our feelings. We know each other well, we trust each other, and we are a good team. The executive training brought me to this place, and for that I am truly thankful.

You can see the heartwarming and forward-propelling energy of gratitude in this example. The manager in question was able to do an amazing job of staying present with this terrible ordeal, and was obviously also doing a great job as a dad. Truth, trust and gratitude were driving forces for showing up with one of the greatest challenges life can throw at us, and he did so with dignity and love.

So we are seeing that gratitude has to be so much more than a concept. It's in your core. When you have something that you have survived, like this, you look outside at the way the sun shines and it's enough. It starts to create a constant state of awe. And if you are operating from that place, you will engage fully with life, and the awe will simultaneously grow.

GRATITUDE EXERCISES

GRATITUDE LIST: This one is very basic, but if you haven't practiced it before, it's an essential starting point. Keep a gratitude list of the top 3 things you are grateful for every day for 3 weeks. There are only 2 rules: (i) You can't write the same things day after day, and (ii) You need to make some attempt to feel the gratitude of the things you are writing about, even if it is only a tiny spark of the feeling. Reflect on how your perspective changes even in this short period of carrying out the exercise.

GRATITUDE MEDITATION: After you've sat in a comfortable position and taken a few deep breaths with your eyes closed, ask yourself, "What am I really grateful for?" The first thing that comes up, play it like a movie in your mind. As you do, feel the waves of gratitude that come from that unfolding. For example, you say to yourself, "I'm thankful for my daughter." You play a video in your mind of reading her a bedtime story, and you feel the waves of gratitude as you watch the video in your mind's eye. Then, "I'm thankful for my mother," and you think of a trip with your mom where you got really close for the first time, and you feel that gratitude within you. You could also work with "What am I grateful for in me? What am I grateful for at work?" Our inner critic shows us how incomplete we are, but we counteract that with gratitude, and we start to see the best in ourselves.

TEAM EXERCISE: You can also practice gratitude exercises with your teams. One exercise we do regularly in our seminars is to sit in a circle with our team and focus on one person at a time. Each person then tells that team member something that is great about them. You start with the sentence, "Jenny, what I find amazing about you is . . ." You let each team member come up with something that they deeply appreciate about each other.

When I lead the team exercise with groups, I usually start by sharing something that happened when I carried out this exercise in a 12-week training program many years ago. It would regularly come up that a group member was not able to attend the session on gratitude with their own group, so they'd ask if they could attend the session with a parallel group who was taking the course on a different night. Typically these attendees would show up in a room full of strangers, and before long, they realized that everyone was going to be giving praise to people they knew, and nobody was going to know who they were. I would then say, "Let's carry out an experiment. There is a huge opportunity in the fact that you don't know this person. Listen to your inner voice and say the first thing that comes to mind about him." Amazingly, the people who had never met him received more bull's-eye comments from him than they did from the people that knew them. In preparation for the session, perhaps they had created a list of what they appreciated about the people they knew, but the visiting person's reference list was non-existent, and they had to rely on their intuition. In this moment they tapped into another way of sensing their environment and the big surprise was how often this was a powerful spot-on remark.

Generally, whenever we carry out the team exercise for gratitude, teams report that it's an amazing experience to sit around and share their gratitude for each other. In my 20 years as a coach, it is extremely rare that I have found teams or environments that say "We regularly show gratitude and give praise." So when we do this exercise, we discuss what it's like to receive praise and what it's like to share it. The overall effect is one of bonding. Sometimes I joke with the group, "Let's be honest, how many of you can raise your hand and say I get so much praise I could puke?!" We establish that it's amazing to receive praise and give it. And we reflect on the fact that most of us don't get enough of it. It reminds me of a joke my wife and I have together: "I told you I loved you when we got married, and I'll let you know when it changes!" We joke about this because we understand that the human condition can be sensitive and fragile and we thrive on reassurance and reminders of our greatness. It brings us to more love and more security, which in turn enables us to operate from a place of safety where we know we are OK. We need to let others know that they are doing great, otherwise they automatically default into assuming the opposite. Focusing on gratitude in this way also takes us out of the ego, which loves to find faults in others. The ego will focus on what is wrong with everyone. "Why is the quality of work so poor?"

"Why is there a typo?" "Why isn't my team working faster?" That is the ego speaking. It's a scarcity mentality. It creates the feeling that others aren't doing enough, or that their quality isn't high enough. Yet when you create the opposite, the whole focus of the team shifts and the energy behind the way they operate changes too.

Now that we've taken one complete journey around the Compass, we're going to spend the final section taking a deeper look at creating a team that is not built on ego, and applying the Inner Compass to some of the typical business scenarios that you will face.

PUTTING IT TOGETHER
APPLYING THE INNER COMPASS

PART 6

CHAPTER 10
THE INNER COMPASS IN BUSINESS

The true test of the Inner Compass work is how you apply it in your everyday business reality. Much of the work that we've done so far with the Inner Compass has involved introspection and a deep look at how you are showing up in the world, both in and out of the workplace. What many leaders find is that there is a transition period between *knowing* the Inner Compass and *living it* in our lives. Like any growth journey, there is always a period where concepts need to be fully lived and integrated, and this is true for Inner Compass leaders too.

Over the years of coaching and mentoring with these tools, both my team and I have identified some common areas where Inner Compass leadership can have the greatest impact in the workplace. So this chapter is going to be very practical. I'll share some common scenarios and we'll look at how the Inner Compass can be used to engineer a completely different approach to both creating positive working cultures and problem-solving in your teams. We'll look at four different scenarios: (1) creating an open and transparent feedback culture, (2) leading change, (3) delegating projects, and (4) budgeting. With each scenario you'll see how the Inner Compass is used in action and you'll see how you can bring these teachings into everyday management situations.

SCENARIO 1 - CREATING AN OPEN AND TRANSPARENT FEEDBACK CULTURE

How do we establish the type of business culture that is characterized by openness, trust and transparency? This is one of the core questions we ask in our Inner Compass leadership journey.

Although much of the work that we have done so far with the Inner Compass is about you, you are probably doing this work mainly because you want to have a fundamentally positive impact on the culture of the workplace. You want to shape and forge the environment around you so that it is not only the most productive, but also so your teams are fulfilled and operating from an optimal mindset. While traditionally many workplaces have been governed by fear, we already learned that fear-based motivations are counterproductive to conscious leadership practices. We want our employees to be open, curious and expansive in their thinking. We want them to relate to their working environment in a way that they feel confident to develop and grow, and trusting enough of the environment that they can make mistakes and learn from them. As their leader, you have the ability to create these kinds of environments, and the key is that without this knowledge and understanding, a lot of workplaces fall into creating habitual and unconscious environments which do not foster the kind of feedback which leads to growth.

One of the core components is a psychologically safe environment where feedback is welcomed. We are aiming to create an atmosphere where individuals and teams enjoy and look forward to receiving feedback, and the opportunity it brings for personal and professional growth. The challenge here is that a lot of feedback in conventional business scenarios throws employees into a survival mindset. Throughout this book, we have referred to the carrot-and-stick mentality that comes with conventional management techniques. Traditionally, feedback has often been used to threaten the safety of an individual's place in an organization. Fear-based tactics can be effective to a certain point. When an individual is guided by fear, they can be more compliant, especially because of the survival mechanisms that get triggered in the brain as they perceive themselves to be in survival. We already discussed how, when an individual feels threatened in the workplace and the survival mode in the brain gets triggered, it sets off a cascading response. Usually, without realizing it, that individual will subconsciously picture a set of images with downward spiraling consequences, and in their mind a series of images will often play out, which may be as extreme as them visualizing losing everything. This kind of catastrophic thinking is common when the survival mindset gets triggered, and if our employees are in that mindset, it often leads to compliant behaviors, which is why those methods of authoritarian-based feedback have been popular in conventional management in the past. However, the downside of this approach—which we have touched upon previously—is that when our employees are in a survival mindset, they are less creative and expansive in their thinking. In short, if we want to create dynamic, forward-thinking teams, one of the most effective ways to achieve that goal is to establish an open and transparent feedback culture.

One of the challenges we will come up against is that many of our employees will likely have already received fear-based feedback. This may have come from previous management. But it may also have come from ourselves. If we've been managing others without being aware of this, we may have inadvertently triggered our employees into survival thinking in the past. And even if this has not come from us, it may have come from other sources within our organization. It can be helpful to assume that some or all of our employees have trigger points around feedback, and with that understanding in mind, the Inner Compass leader adopts a completely different approach to feeding back to employees.

REDUCING FEAR IN THE FEEDBACK PROCESS

In order to create psychological safety in the feedback process, we have to work on reducing fear. We already know that—as human beings—our ego patterns are at the heart of our fears. Our fears sit in the background of the Inner Compass and need to be acknowledged so they can be resolved; otherwise they become our "go-to" safety mechanisms that pull us back into protective ways of behaving. We have been working to identify and resolve your own ego patterns as you move through the Inner Compass, but we also need to acknowledge that your employees have their own ego patterns that will get triggered particularly during feedback.

One way to use the Inner Compass when giving feedback is to sit with the Compass in front of you in preparation for one-on-one conversations with team members. Then ask yourself, "When I am faced with the situation of giving feedback, which element of the Compass pulls me in?" You might say, "I would start with compassion. Everyone is afraid that they won't measure up. That what they have to say isn't good enough. As a result they hold back. By giving them compassion, I feel what they feel. I approach them with more care."

But there is also a way we can go deeper with the Compass and enable it to completely restructure the way we give feedback. One of the more "advanced" ways to use the Compass as managers is to be humble enough to go first with the feedback. With this mindset, a manager will say, "I will do whatever it takes to enable my employees to see that it's OK to make mistakes. I'll be the first one to do it." What we've helped managers to do through coaching them with the Inner Compass is this. "Let's not give employees feedback first. Instead, let's ask them for feedback on us first."

I want to highlight that this isn't an easy path. It takes a certain amount of vulnerability mixed with strength to ask your employees for feedback on you before you give feedback on them. It also turns the conventional leadership approach on its head. But although this can be a challenging path, it is also an opportunity to completely restructure convention, and in doing so, to make choices that can fundamentally change the way your employees operate in the workplace.

You start by asking for their feedback. You can make it anonymous (because again, we don't want to trigger your employees into survival mode by fearing to give constructive criticism of you because there might be consequences). Alternatively you can ask one trusted team member to collect feedback from other team members and collate it. The key is, you want to make sure that your team doesn't feel vulnerable in giving feedback to you, and that you manage it in such a way that it fosters the beginning of an open communication between you and your team.

Ideally you will have already done at least one round of the Inner Compass work before you carry out this exercise. In doing so, you have developed enough of the resilience needed to take constructive criticism, and you are able to acknowledge and work with any ego patterns that this exercise might trigger in you. Then you take the feedback and reflect upon it. Are there any common themes? Is there anything that you would want to start with?

So the next step is to say to yourself, "OK, I can be humble with this feedback." And then to meet with your team and acknowledge what they have highlighted. Perhaps you can say something along the lines of "Thank you for feeding back. This is how you see me, so this is part of my truth now, and I have selected the following to work on. I would like you to give me a couple of months to show progress, and then if you could give me feedback on that, I would appreciate it." This gives your team the chance to recognize that you picked something to work on, and that their feedback was heard. Then a few months down the line, you see how you have done, pick another topic and resolve to work on that.

At this point, when you have shown willingness to take feedback from your team, and have taken the time to get further feedback about the suggestions you have implemented, you can ask, "Would it be OK if we all start giving each other feedback? Who would you like feedback from? At some point I would like to be giving you feedback, just like you gave me." At this stage you've been willing to put your neck out there and been bombarded with stuff you needed to change. You've worked with it, got further feedback and earned their trust. You have also realized how hard it is to work on behavior change and therefore you can meet their future efforts in this area with more understanding and compassion. You've been a role model. So you've earned the kind of trust that has opened your employees to an honest and transparent feedback culture.

At the heart of this process is the willingness to take a risk. There is a trust that you are placing in your team that they will be well-intentioned. There is a humility that comes with the choice to go first. This is why it is so important to have gone around the Compass at least once yourself because you have worked with your own truth and trust and that makes your working with the truth and trust of others more authentic. "I'm willing to be the first one to test if we have psychological safety. If I don't know my truth, how can I work on myself? What is my truth about the way you see me?"

It's also essential that you give this approach time. Even after you've been the role model, it can take time for a team to adapt. What we are essentially doing is supporting our employees to switch the survival mechanism off in their brain. But if this mechanism is strong for some team members, it won't switch off overnight. Some members might question your motivation. Others might think it's a trick. This can be especially true if the Inner Compass methods are a strong contrast to the ones you have used in the past with your team.

When it comes to the time when you're the one giving feedback to team members, it helps to remember to do so from a place of compassion. You might still have someone on the team who is dreading feedback and whose mindset triggers into survival mode at the very thought of that word, so having understanding for that fear is important. But with time and practice, the fear-based mechanisms can be significantly reduced, or even eliminated, and eventually—particularly if you continue to invite feedback from your team about your own growth—team members will welcome a feedback conversation as an opportunity for further development and expansion. What we are ultimately doing here is acknowledging that as human beings our fundamental, core drive is to grow and evolve, and feedback can give us that satisfying feeling of evolution when it is handled with the utmost respect and care.

SCENARIO 2 - LEADING CHANGE

Any seasoned manager will tell you that one of the biggest challenges an organization faces is implementing change projects. In the earlier days of my coaching career, I supported management teams to implement change projects, particularly around a new business strategy that required a lot of change. These more old-school methods of leading change would include a kickoff event. This was a well-rehearsed process—a performance almost—that would *sell the employees on change*. The reasoning behind this is that in a common business scenario, change is often feared. It is another area that can trigger employees into survival mode and the fear that fundamental company change will lead to a loss of employment or status. So the kickoff event would be a way to raise the positive expectations of the employees and convince them about the change ahead.

As time went on I started to question the way that these kickoff events are structured and delivered—particularly the intentionality behind them. I asked myself, "What's the intention here? To sell people on the necessity of change. And what's our expectation of those in the audience? Are we expecting them to voice their opinions or is this showmanship a way of ensuring they keep their mouths shut?" I began to question the very foundation that these kickoff events were built upon.

First of all, the leadership team would stand on stage with a finely tuned powerpoint presentation. There would usually be banners and other branding paraphernalia. The management team would be dressed for the occasion. The speech would have been rehearsed and then delivered in such a way that it would appear that the management team knew exactly what was about to happen, and it would seem from an audience perspective that the management knew the way. Yet a significant portion of change projects fails to achieve the initially expected results. If you think about it, it can only be the ego that puts on a show and says, "We know the way. Follow us." And if you are one of the hundreds of people in the room, why would you dare speak up in a moment like this? Essentially, the people in the audience are being asked to challenge information they are seeing for the first time, in front of many people, *including senior management.* If your valuable team members have doubts about a change project, wouldn't you want them to speak up? Yet the setup of those old-school events isn't geared towards that, but more towards supporting the ego's need to feel safe.

One of the basic elements of those events is the one-way communication. And a fundamental challenge with one-way communications is that, if you don't create a viable way for your employees to communicate their concerns, they will do it in small groups around the office, which will foster further fear and mistrust, and create an "us and them" mentality between employees and management. When we close the channels of communication in change projects, we are asking for an environment where our teams are split between what they hear in public, and what they say in private. This creates the antithesis of an honest and open working environment.

These days, when my team and I coach big change projects, we share a contrasting method to the more conventional approach. A lot of this comes down to the "why" behind the change, and to approach the project with a more humble emphasis.

The approach for this would be something along the lines of "We are about to show you why we need to make a change. We are going to share some of the ideas that we have, but I would be misleading you if I said any of us knows how it's going to play out exactly. There will be periods of chaos and discomfort. At times we might feel like we are lost. But I am confident that if we keep an open dialogue and correct our mistakes quickly, we can get there together."

If you think about this approach from an Inner Compass perspective, we are touching upon several different elements of the Compass at one time. The first is truth and the acknowledgment that we don't know the answers. The second is humility and the fact that I—as your leader—don't have all the answers either. The third is trust and the acknowledgment that, if we have an open dialogue, we'll find the way. The fourth is intention, particularly the intention to engage employees and get them on board with the plan. The fifth is purpose, and the why behind the change. We'll break each of these elements down in relation to the Inner Compass.

It's usually possible to show why we need to change. However, as soon as people see there might be headcount reductions, they can be triggered into survival mode and that "us and them" mentality between employees and management is established. The dialogue that goes with this resistance is usually something like "They are stuffing their pockets with more profit. They are letting people go because they are unfair. They are doing this so there will be more money at the top of the food chain." However, most of the time these assumptions are not correct. Companies gain fat over time because nobody was honest enough. The competitive edge was lost. So a need develops to streamline operations. Not because the management wants to be mean to the few people they are letting go, but because they want to protect the people they are keeping.

Here, we have the elements of truth and humility mixed together. The truth is that we don't have all the answers, and when we communicate this to our teams, we bring in humility at the same time by admitting, "We are going to make mistakes."

We then bring in the elements of trust when we share, "I am convinced that if we put our heads together, there are enough bright heads to find the way."

Intention also plays a part: My intention is to get everyone involved in finding the way forward. With a further intention of securing a healthy workplace for years to come.

If you let the Inner Compass guide you, it takes you beyond ego. In the past, I have heard those I coach resist this approach at first: "There are 2000 people in my company, I have to look strong, even if it means I have to fake it till I make it." But the Inner Compass approaches are taking us to a more humanitarian approach to management. One that simultaneously acknowledges that change can be challenging for people and supports them to navigate it to the best of their ability.

With this approach, there is a level of brutal honesty that you have to be OK with. The Inner Compass is not soft because truth is not soft either. As an Inner Compass leader, you need to be willing to take a stand. Just as in the first section of this chapter where we talked about a new way to approach feedback in your teams, you were willing to say, "I am the way I am. You see sides of me that are not clear to me. When you point those out to me, I will understand myself even better. Thank you for being open and honest in your feedback to me." Adapting to change in the company is also similar. You are basically saying, "Let's face it. None of us have all the answers. We need to stay in dialogue so we can figure them out together." And once you start that dialogue, trust and compassion become crucial. We encourage managers to walk around in their companies and ask, "How is the change working out? Can I help you with any aspect of it?" And to also create focus groups that directly ask, "How's the change going? Where can we do better?" Then to follow up in town hall meetings: "I spoke to Jimmy in the warehouse and Sarah in sales. I learned about our mistakes and I am correcting them now. I'll keep you updated on the progress of those corrections. Keep me informed if there are other aspects that we need to address."

To summarize this section on leading change: if we take the traditional kickoff approach, mistakes start on the stage. We have top-down communication and because we are not in dialogue, we make assumptions and close down communication further. What we need instead are ongoing conversations about people's worries and insecurities. We need trust for what they bring to the conversation, we need to acknowledge their concerns and show compassion when they express them. We need to be humble in our acceptance and truthful in our response. Then, and only then, can we lead change in the most human-centered way.

SCENARIO 3 - DELEGATING PROJECTS

The Inner Compass can also be an incredibly powerful tool when it comes to delegating projects. One of the first questions we deal with is why we are delegating. We can summarize some common reasons for delegation as follows:

1. The workload is unevenly distributed. I have too much on my plate and I need to delegate, free up more time, and even the distribution.
2. There is one person in the company who knows how to do this task, but if they leave, or anything happens to them, nobody else knows how to do it, so I need a backup.
3. There's an employee that really needs to grow, and delegating will support their growth in that particular area.

Any focus on delegating needs to begin with truth and purpose. You'll need to begin with clarity around why you're delegating and then you can deliver the truth to the employees involved with complete transparency. So, what's the purpose of delegating and what's the truth behind the situation? We can look at it in the following scenario.

Let's say you have a delegation opportunity for a really important project in the company—one that's going to bring a lot of kudos and growth opportunities for the candidate that you choose. There are three candidates in your mind. You consider Jeff, the new guy, but you aren't sure if he has enough experience to take this project on. There's Johnny—his ego is pretty big and he is likely the one that expects to be the first in line for this project. But Alexia is a strong contender too, and it's pretty likely that Johnny will not take it well if she gets nominated. His ego's going to be bruised and it might affect his other projects. You're going to benefit from using both truth and purpose from the Compass to handle this situation carefully and successfully.

REFLECTION POINT: Starting with purpose, what's the purpose of delegating from your point of view? How is this decision going to affect you as a manager? Get clear on the purpose of the delegation before you proceed.

When you have clarity on the purpose of the delegation, you can move into taking action. It's going to be helpful if you can be humble, vulnerable and open as you start to speak to the various team members to test the water and make sure the delegation of this project lands properly. Something along the lines of "I'm looking to delegate this and I haven't yet decided who I'm going to delegate it to yet. You're one of three candidates I have in mind and I would like to have a conversation with you about it. I don't have all the answers to be able to tell you right now, but I'd like to open the discussion with you." Simultaneously, you are going to be looking for opportunities to demonstrate appropriate vulnerability. If you are truthful, humble and vulnerable in the way you communicate, you open the way for others to behave in the same way. In addition, you can meet each team member where they are. You can show compassion to Johnny who feels his specialness is being taken away if he isn't the only one in line for the project. You can explore Jeff as the new team member and be open and curious about the potential skills that he is bringing to the table. You can coach Alexia and let her know that you have confidence in her ability to potentially carry this project forward. All those who were considered should be able to say, "I did have an open and honest conversation with my boss about this project and it was a fair and transparent selection process." And consequently, no employee is left with the feeling of "I was never really consulted about this process."

OVERT USE OF THE INNER COMPASS

In the above example, we used the Inner Compass covertly to guide the way you communicate with your employees. But another angle is to use the Inner Compass as a more overt tool that you directly apply with your employees. For example:

> **You:** OK Alexia, I'm thinking about getting you on board. Let's get together to look at the Inner Compass. What's the truth about how you are feeling? Let's look at the Compass and see where it pulls you in.
>
> **Alexia:** It pulls me into trust because I'm not sure if the team trusts me to carry out this task.

So in this instance the Compass will give Alexia an opportunity to open up to the vulnerability that she is feeling and give you an opportunity to talk through her fears with her. In the end, you choose Alexia. Further conversations with her might include:

> **You:** Alexia I'm going to delegate this to you, what are you aware of?"

Alexia: That I might make mistakes and that the team wouldn't forgive me.

You: And what kind of support do you need to move through this fear so that you can step up?

And you can then use the combination of compassion, awareness and action to discuss how she can move forward.

The core thing to remember is that the answers that your employees give you are going to be an insight into their own patterns and programs. What we are creating here is an environment where you openly acknowledge that we all have patterns and programs that guide our perspectives. In conventional business scenarios, these patterns are not usually discussed openly. In some cases they may be seen as weaknesses or flaws. But an Inner Compass leader takes a different approach. We allow our employees to acknowledge these patterns and then we support them to move beyond them. It's not that we are acting as a therapist to our employees. It's more that we become a skillful coach who has taken time to become aware of their own patterns and develops the skills to help others acknowledge and move through theirs. Like any good coach, your role here will be to see your employees' potential beyond their own perceived limitations, and to support them to realize that potential. Then you develop a dynamic team that has faith in you and your ability to not only see the best in them, but also to help them to develop their potential.

Simultaneously, and particularly if you considered several candidates for a delegated position, how you feed back to the employees that you didn't choose is as important as how you feed back to those you did select. You'll need to handle with sensitivity and care the potential disappointments from those who weren't chosen to take this project forward. And as you do that, you can focus on their skills rather than their deficits.

Your dialogue might sound something like this:

> **You:** Johnny, you are a highly valuable asset and someone I can really rely on for a project like this one. On this occasion, I have selected Alexia to take this project forward because there are skills I'd like her to develop. I'm looking forward to working with you on future projects. Are there any particular skills you would like to develop so that I can keep that in mind for further collaborations with you?

And to Jeff:

> **You:** Jeff, I'm really glad to have you on board. I've selected Alexia for this project as there are particular skills that she has that I am supporting her to develop. I'd like to do the same with you on future projects when you've had more time to settle in here. Are there any particular skills you are looking to develop so that I can factor that into future decisions?

You will also want to be able to back up the promises that you make so that those that didn't get the opportunity this time can see that you were genuine about opportunities in the future.

SCENARIO 4 - BUDGETING

Another use of the Compass can be found in planning and budgeting for the next year of business.

Before we look at how to use the Compass for this task, take a moment to reflect on how budgeting usually goes. It doesn't matter what country you are in or what company you work for: when it comes to planning, you are most likely asked to deliver your numbers from the bottom up.

Ordinarily, you know they will cut your budget. So you buffer it. It's what you've been trained to do. But this is not really an Inner Compass way. Instead, it's an ego way. It's a dysfunctional game that we've all been taught to play in conventional business scenarios. This cost cutting and buffering means that nobody is allowed to live their truth. Both sides are playing poker, and we enter a world where nobody is truthful. This time-consuming, stressful, and untruthful approach needs to end for all of us, and we can use the Compass to transform the way we budget from now on.

For budgeting from an Inner Compass perspective, we get the ego out of the way, and we start with truth and purpose. We need the purpose of planning and budgeting and the truth about how we are currently performing. We also need the truth about the market we are operating in. Both sides need to agree on this truth. You need to have fostered a relationship of trust with the senior management team so that when they get your proposed numbers, they have faith in them. But this works both ways. You need the trust of your team too. If there is a bonus system in place and your team maxes it out with minimum effort, you lose trust in them, or if it is unfair or ineffective, they will lose trust in you. So trust needs to be present on both sides.

You may remember that in Part Two of this book, I highlighted that trust is such a core element of the Compass that when I did my first speech on it, one audience member told me, "Interesting concept but you only need truth and trust." It's very much core. And you may also remember the religious guy that I presented to who said, "In the middle of the Compass you should have faith, and that faith is a combination of truth and trust." We previously highlighted that you can call these elements the heartbeat of the Compass. And while we already covered these concepts extensively in earlier chapters, when it comes to tasks like budgeting, you can really see them come to life.

I have an example of how to use this in action from my early days of leadership when I managed the Icelandic Broadcasting Sales Team (which was mentioned earlier in this book). We had a good year behind us, and I got the message that a 15 percent sales increase might be dropped upon us. I instantly knew that this was not going to go down well with the team. I thought about how we could have a fairer chance. So I said to them, "Budgeting time will come soon, and I would like us to be thorough." Everyone met me individually for a long working lunch, and I asked each of them: "We still haven't been given the numbers for next year, but if we did everything right, what would be possible (in currency)?"

The whole atmosphere was very upbeat. We approached it with the mindset of "Let's see what we can do." One team member shared, "Well, my client has a new line they are launching and this should increase their potential for further investment." The economy was booming and most of them landed between a 20 to 30 percent increase. I shared with them, "It's probably not wise to promise more than a 20 percent increase. Shall we aim for 15 percent just to be safe?" So they got to that place of seeing the potential of increase on their own. This was where some of my earlier understandings of how to motivate a team beyond ego pressures came from. If we approached this from an ego stance, they would never have taken a fair look at the options. They would have been triggered into defensive mode and would have reacted from that place. So, when it comes to planning and budgeting, we have to free ourselves from the defensive reactions which are linked to survival and fear of failure. Instead, as a team, we need to approach budgeting with the mindset of "If we were to do everything right, what could be possible for us?" It's a more expansive approach which opens us up to possibilities, instead of shutting us down with fear.

REFLECTION POINT: How would you approach budgeting from an Inner Compass perspective? Which elements of the Compass speak to you and guide you on where to start?

As more and more companies evolve the way they approach budgeting, we are seeing trends of moving away from individual bonus systems and looking at the bigger picture. There is an increasing attitude of "Either we all do well or nobody does well." In conventional scenarios, when only the salespeople make a fortune, they are treated like gods, and it's the perfect territory for ego and status. We can't have that kind of approach and simultaneously be Inner Compass leaders. It has to go in the direction of "If we really believe in cooperation and collaboration and being one family, we need to put our money where our mouth is."

From these four examples we can see how the Inner Compass is an experiential path in common business scenarios, and how it can take you beyond ego into what's possible.

CONCLUSION

I We started our Inner Compass journey together with the intention of leading beyond our egos. As you are reading this, you have likely gone around the Compass at least once, and you may have even worked your way around it several times. As we highlighted in chapter 1, the Inner Compass is designed so that each time you go around it, you expand and grow more, both as a leader and in your life outside the workplace.

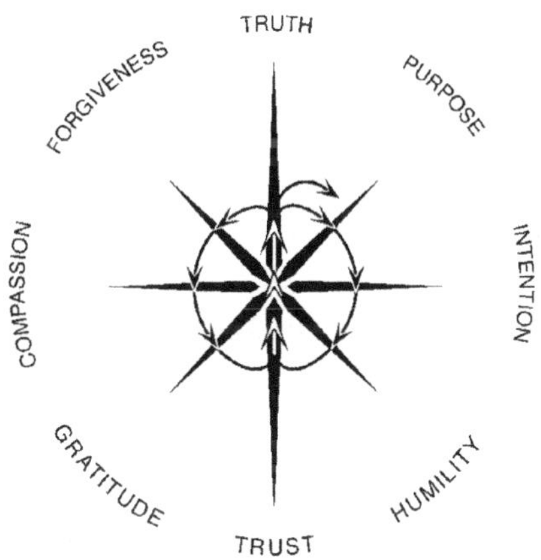

One thing that I hope that you are gaining from this work, if you are leaning in deeply, is the sense that there is no end point or destination to this journey that we are on together. If you recall, in the opening chapter, I highlighted that we can see conscious leadership as a kind of spectrum where, on one end we are completely lost in our ego and our patterns, and ruling from a place of fear. And on the other end we are conscious of our actions, humble and compassionate, and willing to learn from our mistakes so that we can grow. One of the biggest challenges of working with the ego is that, if we temporarily experience a point where we are on the fully conscious end of the spectrum, it can present us with the feeling that we have reached a final destination and ironically, that is often the point where we stagnate and stop growing.

In reality, the nature of our human existence means that when we grow, it is never a fixed or static experience, and new challenges will highlight new growth edges, most likely until our final days. We might see periods of relative ease, but we will also likely see tumultuous periods which will bring significant growth opportunities if we navigate them in the most effective way.

The Inner Compass is designed to be a path that is always available to us and that we can count on at all times. We can get the sense that we are "never alone" and that we always have our special path to follow so that we can question ourselves, and look for openings for growth. This means that we can lead in the most powerful yet humble way, with our hearts open, and with the possibility that even our greatest challenges can be met with gratitude, compassion and the willingness to step into our greatness—beyond our ego—in any given moment.

Here's to a world filled with leaders like yourself who are willing to look into their patterns and to lead from beyond ego, to build a more conscious business world, and ultimately, a sustainable life for our planet as a whole.

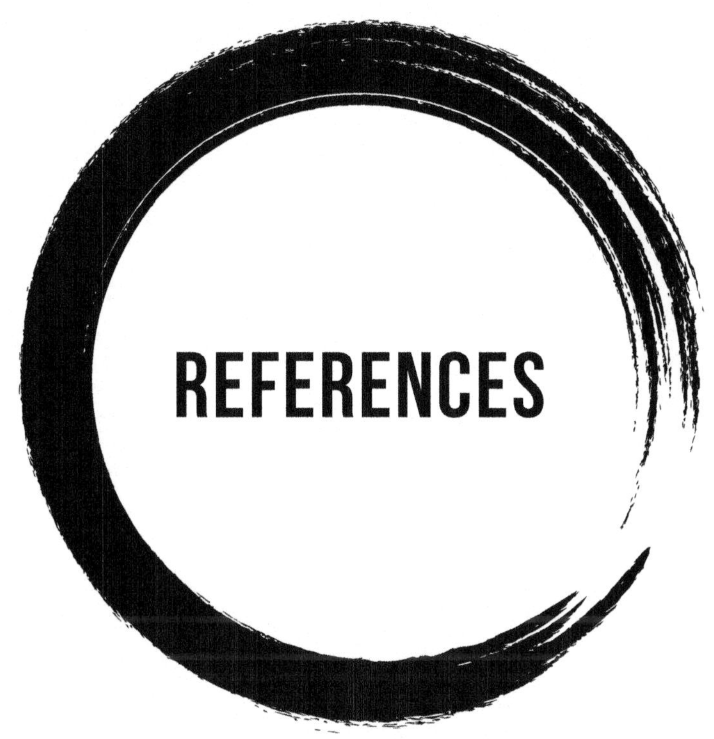

CHAPTER 1

1. https://rework.withgoogle.com/print/guides/5721312655835136/
2. https://rework.withgoogle.com/print/guides/5721312655835136/
3. https://www.youtube.com/watch?v=LhoLuui9gX8

CHAPTER 3

1. https://advisory.kpmg.us/insights/future-hr/future-hr-purpose-culture/kpmg-purpose.html
2. https://china.jdpower.com/en/resources/smartphone-connectivity-now-most-common-problem-cited-new-vehicle-owners-jd-power-finds

CHAPTER 8

1. https://www.youtube.com/watch?v=uRcOH4SnfbM

RESOURCES

FOR MORE INFORMATION ON THE INNER COMPASS OR TO WORK WITH THOR OLAFSSON & HIS TEAM, PLEASE VISIT: **WWW.BEYONDEGO.COM**

THANKS

Heartfelt gratitude goes to my wife and soulmate Svava Björk for providing endless moral support during the trying time of writing a book that means so much, as well as to my writing partner and friend Sasha Allenby for her genius ability to give words to the Inner Compass.

I also thank my friend and business partner Chris Atkinson for always being available with support and advice, Kate Tuck for her soulful design of the cover, Lois Rose for her wonderful editing work and Cosima Raschendorfer, Anne Mench and the entire team at the Strategic Leadership companies for their patience and support while waiting for this work to be born.

Others who supported the process of bringing forth the messages of the Inner Compass and who receive my sincere thanks are: Mammad Mahmoodi, Joel Beverly, Dr. Frank Schlein, Hörður Arnarson, Halla Tómasdóttir, Mike Dennett, Ian Smith, Joachim Herr, Ingrid Kuehtz, Guo Wei, Werner Eikenbush, Eric Malitzke, Jónína S. Lárusdóttir, Birgir Jónsson, Vaishali Ahuja, Joan Halifax, Helga Halldórsdóttir, Mark Makowski, Sveinn Hróbjartsson, Krishna Reddy, Asgeir Jonsson and Dr. Marsha King.

Thor Olafsson is passionate about supporting leaders to heighten their levels of consciousness, so that they can lead from within. He has been an award-winning leadership coach and consultant for over 20 years, and has worked across 30 countries and 5 continents. Some of his key clients through the years have included Arion Bank, BMW Group, Bertelsmann, Central Bank of Iceland, Continental and Roche Diagnostics, to name a few.

Thor founded several companies in four different countries, before deciding to concentrate all his efforts on his group of Strategic Leadership companies. He currently has a team of over 40 executive coaches and leadership trainers in countries around the globe. He specializes in coaching senior teams on becoming conscious strategic leaders, as well as working individually with top-level executives. He works with CEOs and MDs, as well as managers who are being fast-tracked towards a higher level of responsibility.

Thor developed an effective coaching and training framework called the Inner Compass, which is highly praised by senior executives. With this body of work, Thor and his team have launched a global platform called www.beyondego.com, a non-profit initiative that provides leaders with the resources and tools to lead from beyond their egos. He believes that the time is right for the corporate world to wake up to unconscious patterns and become true conscious leaders, leading the world into a more humane and sustainable future.